THE RED LIGHT ZONE

AN INSIDER'S 'LAUGH 'N' TELL' OF BBC RADIO

JEFF ZYCINSKI

THE LUNICORN PRESS

THE LUNICORN PRESS LTD

Scotland

Text © Jeff Zycinski 2019

All rights reserved

First published 2019 by The Lunicorn Press Ltd.

1

Printed by Martins the Printers, Berwick-upon-Tweed
Designed and typeset by Heather Macpherson at
Raspberry Creative Type
Cover Artwork © Emma McGregor 2019

British Library Cataloguing in Publication Data
A CIP catalogue record for this book is available from the
British Library

ISBN: 978-0-9929264-6-5

To Anne, Sarah and Alan ... and Rascal

PRAISE FOR
THE RED LIGHT ZONE

"As well as chronicling his time at BBC Radio
Scotland, Zycinski offers amusement, bemusement
and some honest reflections on the work. The book
is interesting for all these reasons, but also because
it paints a portrait of a man who loves his radio
and whose heart lives for creative and inventive
programme making."

Liveanddeadly.net

ACKNOWLEDGEMENTS

Huge thanks to Lyn McNicol and Laura Jackson at Lunicorn Press, who encouraged me to write this little book, and kept me on the straight and narrow throughout the process. Also, thanks to my editor, Gale Winskill. Emma McGregor provided the photography and artwork and Heather Macpherson designed the cover and the overall look of the book. Richard Melvin at Dabster gave me permission to reproduce lyrics from 'Santa's a Scotsman'; he's owed some Brussels sprouts.

Special thanks to all friends and former colleagues who answered my queries about past events and helped me put things in the right order. I'm sure some of the chronology is out of kilter, but we'll call that poetic licence rather than my senility.

By and large people and events recalled in this book are done so with respect, affection and just sometimes, a bit of cheekiness. Some stories I omitted because I suspected the people involved might get huffy or hunt me down. If, on the other hand, you were hoping to get a mention, but did not, you can start that campaign for a sequel. Now that I no longer work for the BBC, I am open to bribes, political coercion and brazen product placement. Tunnock's!

CONTENTS

PREFACE:
AN APOLOGY

The Red Light Zone? Yes, I know. It's a bit misleading, isn't it? I'm sorry if you picked up this book thinking it was an edgy exposé of Amsterdam brothels, Edinburgh massage parlours or Lochwinnoch tearooms (we've all heard the stories). But no – it's all about radio, which is sexy in its own way of course. Just be thankful that we didn't follow through with the original idea we had for the front cover: I was to be photographed in a miniskirt, leaning into a car window as I tried to persuade some hapless punter to change the station on his car radio and try a bit of hard-core current affairs, or a quickie comedy sketch. I'm not saying those photographs don't exist; I'm just saying there are ideas you have after a few drinks and they don't always seem so brilliant when you see the prints.

We had mulled over other titles for this book. I reminded my friend and former Radio Scotland presenter, Tom

Morton, that he had once suggested that any memoir of BBC Scotland should be entitled *Up Auntie's Kilt*. He had no memory of this but gave me permission to steal it. I fell in love with this title for a few weeks but then dumped it on the grounds that no one I'd worked with had ever referred to the BBC as 'Auntie'. That term of endearment only ever appears in newspaper articles written by the kind of reporters who also describe scientists as 'boffins' and who still say 'double-U, double-U, double-U' when recommending a website.

Next, we considered *A Head for Radio*, thinking it would be a neat wordplay on my former job title as 'Head of Radio' at BBC Scotland, as well as alluding to some vague psychological angle. In the end though it sounded too much like one of those BBC policy documents from the 1970s: 'Ahead for Radio: Public Broadcasting for the Twentieth Century'.

So it's *The Red Light Zone* because much of my career has been spent in soundproof studios where the red light signifies a live microphone and a reminder not to cough, sneeze, swear or blurt out any honest thoughts about the Government, opposition parties, Ofcom, the BBC Director General, awards committees, football teams, bishops, needy comedians, psychotic agents, BBC accountants, overpaid presenters, moaning journalists, television producers and accordionists. Now that I'm no longer one of Auntie's nephews (damn it!) the red light is off and I can say what I like about all of those things.

The only snag is that after twenty-five years at the BBC I've become conditioned to holding my tongue. This came home to me after I announced my departure plans and a friend invited me to join his particular political party and maybe stand for election.

'Trouble is,' I told him, 'I've worked for the BBC for so long I don't know what my opinions are any more.'

'That needn't be a problem,' he assured me. 'We can supply the opinions.'

Ah, so that's how it works.

In the meantime, let me tell you how I sold my body and mind to broadcasting and about the people I met, the places I visited and the programmes we made. Friends have asked if this is going to be one of those 'kiss 'n' tell' memoirs, but I don't think my air-kissing encounters with luvvies would justify that description. However, there were lots of laughs, so maybe 'laugh 'n' tell' is more appropriate. There are also movie stars, one car chase and some nudity. Not much sex though.

Again, sorry about that.

1.

THIS IS HOW IT ENDS

There was still no word back from Sean Connery, but the BBC lawyer said we were good to go and I called the Drama Department and gave them the word. *The Fountainbridge Spy*, a fictional imagining of how an Edinburgh milkman had landed the part of James Bond, would be a centrepiece of Radio Scotland's Christmas schedule. I had written to the famous actor, telling him about the play and asking him to consider a cameo appearance, but there had been no reply. It had always been a long shot.

I now turned to the image on my computer screen. It was a pastiche of the Beatles' *Sergeant Pepper* album cover, but in our version, all the famous figures were those whose voices would feature during the station's winter season of programmes. Billy Connolly stood next to Sheena Easton and Sharleen Spiteri; J.K. Rowling peeped out above members of Deacon Blue; Robbie Coltrane looked like the fifth member of Wet, Wet, Wet.

I shouted over to James Christie, our social-media producer. He was sitting at the next bank of desks, working out how to animate the whole thing on the station's website and Facebook page. I told him that James Bond could now be added, so 007 was duly inserted into the front row with his gun pointing over the head of Rab C. Nesbitt. Oor Wullie would have to be removed, however, as there were some copyright complications with *The Sunday Post's* famous cartoon strip.

'Jings!' said James.

'Michty me,' I replied.

I called David Treasurer in our marketing department. He would be making the radio trails for the season and was waiting to hear what should be included. It was always odd to be talking about winter programmes at the fag end of the summer, but this kind of forward-planning was part of the job. The *Radio Times* demanded billings information weeks in advance and all the production departments wanted to know if they would be making extra programmes. If we were planning a live show for Hogmanay, for example, the music producers would have to start booking bands: musicians were always in demand at that time of year and if you left it too late, you'd be lucky to snap up one of those buskers who played the harmonica to cinema queues.

'Bond is in, but Wullie's out,' I told David.

'Jings!' he replied, 'Michty me and help ma boab.'

'Yes, we've done all that.'

As I ended the call, I saw that Irene Jones, my PA, was trying to catch my attention.

'The boss wants to see you.'

6

I looked at my watch. It was after four o'clock. I had planned a curry night with the radio management team and was hoping to get away sharply.

'When?' I asked.

'Right now.'

That didn't sound good. I pulled on my jacket, straightened my tie and walked down to the third floor. Donalda MacKinnon, Director of BBC Scotland, was sitting in one of the glass-walled meeting rooms near her desk. As I drew closer, I saw Elaine from HR making a quick exit and disappearing down the back stairs. Usually she would make eye contact and say a quick 'hello'. Not this time. This was not good at all.

When the boss calls you into her office and tells you that your job is being scrapped, it's probably not a good idea to threaten her with sabotage – sabotage involving banjos, no less, but I'll get to that. Take it from me, as someone who studied psychology for four years (and whose party piece as a student was feigning interest in people's daft dreams), I know all about the Kübler-Ross Change Curve and the Five Stages of Grief: denial, anger, bargaining, depression and acceptance. These were originally observed in terminally ill patients as doctors broke the bad news and suggested they shouldn't start following a new storyline in their favourite soap.

In theory, the whole process leading to 'acceptance' can take weeks or even months, but in my case, I cycled through all five stages within the space of that half-hour meeting. Donalda had offered tea and engaged in a few minutes of small talk before steeling herself and getting to the point. She was a good boss, one of the best I'd ever had, and I could see this was difficult for her. She had been very open about her plans to change the management structure and create a clear separation between programme production and programme commissioning. This had been tried before at the BBC – more than once – but if you worked for the Corporation long enough you saw the same ideas, structures, problems and sandwiches come around again and again. Nevertheless, Donalda was determined to press on with her plan.

She took a deep breath and told me there would not, in future, be a Head of Radio. This should have shocked me because there was only one Head of Radio at BBC Scotland and I was it. In fact, I had been 'it' for the past twelve years – almost half the length of my career at the BBC. I even uttered the words 'I'm shocked', because that felt like the right thing to say.

In hindsight I wish I had chosen that moment to steal from the sitcom character Frasier Crane and exclaim in the style of a bad Shakespearian actor, 'I … am … wounded!'

I didn't. What I really felt at that late hour in the afternoon was hunger, but 'I'm hungry' would have been an inappropriate response. I wasn't shocked because for the previous three months it had been me explaining to Donalda that her new structure didn't allow for a Head of Radio, or for any one individual with responsibility for both the production teams that made the programmes, alongside the authority to decide which programmes should be made. She was splitting the buyers from the sellers, so no one could be both.

I'd argued this point in the manner of a pre-Christmas turkey who unfurls the tinfoil and offers its own recipe for the stuffing. Finally, she'd seen it my way. So what if I was about to lose my job, status, income and free copy of the *Radio Times*? At least I'd won the argument. Future ambitions were foiled. Fetch the cranberry sauce, someone.

Or maybe not, because Donalda was known for her honesty and integrity and I believed her as she told me how much I was valued and how she hoped I would stick around. True, she couldn't yet tell me what my job might be in the future, that would have to be worked out; no, there wasn't a fixed timescale for these changes. Meantime it would be business as usual. Well, apart from the pesky job-loss business, of course.

As I often do in tense situations, I attempted to lighten the mood with a bit of humour. I reminded her that the following day, I would be over at the City Halls in Glasgow, working with the BBC Scottish Symphony Orchestra as they recorded a new set of musical stings, themes, beds and idents for the radio station. We'd been working on this for almost a year. A composer had been commissioned and the orchestra would add that element of class and style to the station sound. The new package would be launched in November, on St Andrew's Day, to coincide with Radio Scotland's thirty-ninth birthday.

'Given your bombshell news,' I told Donalda, maintaining my facial expression in its natural resting state of surliness, 'I now have great scope for sabotage.'

She looked at me, confused and slightly worried. 'I might ask them to include banjos.'

She gave me a smile that was credit-card thin and I brought her misery to an end by standing up, thanking her for her time and telling her that this might just be the kick up the backside I needed after almost twenty-five years at the Beeb.

Bravado and dignity, I thought. Besides, I had arranged that curry night and I was already in pre-gorging salivation mode. So, I walked away and, change curve be damned, I already knew what I wanted to do next.

Escape.

Let's face it: being told that my job was gone was a bit of a hint that I may have outstayed my welcome. There seemed to me no point in hanging around or taking one of those made-up project-management roles that the BBC invents when someone is determined to cling on by their fingernails; Creative Dispersal Lead, for example – a title I've just plucked out of thin air, but I had better check that it doesn't exist.

I'd enjoyed my time at the BBC and it had lasted a lot longer than I had ever expected. I liked the people, enjoyed the creativity and had opportunities to travel the length and breadth of Scotland, and even beyond. I had worked in radio and television; had made serious documentaries and light-hearted features, invented quiz shows and debate formats; I had commissioned drama, performed stand-up comedy, gatecrashed millionaires' parties and met many heroes and villains along the way.

I was reminded of a speech I used to give to production trainees as part of their induction week. After telling them how they should seize every opportunity the BBC had to offer, I reflected on the disgruntled minority of BBC staffers who would sit and complain about their lot and wait for management to sort out their lives. These tended to be people who had never worked for anyone else except the

BBC and who, even if the world's top obstetrician had presented them with irrefutable evidence, did not know they were born.

'Promise me this,' I would tell the trainees, 'if you get to a point in your BBC career where you are no longer enjoying it, then do yourself a favour and leave. We'll do all we can to help you find opportunities elsewhere, but don't sit in here dragging everyone else down. Please leave.'

It was time to take my own advice.

It's been said that when someone finally exits the BBC (much like when anyone quits any big organisation) the hole that they leave behind seals itself just as soon as they drive out of the car park. People move on. They have to. All the same, I appreciated the messages I received from colleagues with whom I had crossed paths (and sometimes swords) over the years. I was equally amused by those who asked if there was some kind of scandal prompting my decision. Had I, for example, pocketed one of the Children in Need collecting tins? Had my numerous expense claims for chocolate muffins finally come to the attention of auditors? Had someone finally unearthed copies of those old student magazines and discovered that article I'd written about the Pope? A little more unsettling were those messages from people inside and outside the BBC who wanted to know if my departure had opened up a job vacancy. Steal my grave as fast, why don't you?

Of all the questions I was asked in my final months, two were voiced most often: 'What are you going to do next?' and 'How did you get started in radio in the first place?'

So, what I'm going to do next is answer the second question first. Does that make sense? No? Oh, do try to keep up. There are strippers in the next chapter ... dolphins too.

2.

STRIPPERS AND DOLPHINS

My professional career in radio began in 1988 in a Soho strip club. I was fully clothed. The Paul Raymond Revue Bar styled itself as 'The World Centre of Erotic Entertainment' and was, for a time, one of the few legal venues in London offering full-frontal nudity to paying customers. Having completed my Social Sciences degree in Glasgow, I was now a post-graduate student at the Centre for Journalism Studies in Cardiff. It was one of the top three journalism courses in Britain and drew its fair share of Oxbridge graduates, many of whom became close friends. Fellow students included Juliette Dwyer, who went on to be an Editor in charge of the BBC's fact-checking unit, and Heather Bosch, who became an award-winning anchor with CBS in New York.

Somehow, I had parlayed a portfolio of my student magazine articles into a reasonable application and was thrilled to have been accepted. A few months into the course, we had a visit from two important bods from Capital Radio in London. They brought with them a reel of quarter-inch tape, looped it through the big Studer machine in our training studio and we sat in awe, listening to a superbly crafted documentary on homelessness which demonstrated the potential of voices, sounds and music. It not only told a story, it transported us to different locations via different emotions. Twelve of us on the Broadcast Journalism module had spent weeks learning to operate faders, mark tape with a soft chinagraph pencil and splice it on a metal editing block, to get our Teeline shorthand speed up to 100 words per minute and write essays on libel law and the ethics of reporting. This masterclass by people working in the industry made it all come alive. They then revealed their hidden agenda: Capital Radio was going to make a special programme to mark that year's 'Leap Day' – 29th February – and would tell, using only audio, the story of a 'Day in the Life of London'.

Their own team of reporters would be augmented by students from institutions like ours, and each of us would be given a particular assignment in a pre-arranged location. The idea was that we should not *interview* people but attempt to record 'actuality' from the scene: sounds, noises and snippets of conversations that would happen on any normal day. The instruction was to blend into the background rather than brandish microphones in faces. This all sounded like great fun and on the day itself, I was told I had the look of someone who could comfortably lurk in the shadows of a seedy strip club and so I was sent to Soho.

From early morning until midnight I tried to make myself as invisible as possible as I tiptoed from the box office, where Japanese businessmen demanded to know the bar prices – 'How much for gin?' – before buying a ticket, to the backstage area, where a carpenter was boasting about all the famous theatres where he had wielded his saw and hammer – 'London Palladium, Drury Lane, done 'em all, mate.' Most poignant was the steady stream of young women turning up at the door and asking for an audition. On that day, all were given a quick once-over and turned away before they got further than the foyer. There was also an annoying bouncer who had been instructed to keep an eye on me and who kept leaning into my microphone shouting, 'He can't wait to see the naked girls!' In truth, I was quite nervous about seeing the naked girls, not because of my youthful shyness, but because I couldn't figure out how I could translate nudity into audio.

So, if I remember anything from that night it was about me peering at the recording-level meter on my Sony Walkman Pro as topless girls marched on stage dressed, to some extent, as American footballers. There was no commentary to help me paint my audio picture, just the music that provided the beat for the dancing and the discarding of costumes – and the appreciative applause of gin-soaked Japanese businessmen. This was augmented by a few American-style hoots and hollers, but then the annoying bouncer came to my rescue. He appeared by my side and with a voice dripping with sleaze began to mouth creepy descriptions of each girl on the stage, alongside a pithy critique of their dancing abilities.

'Nice bum; two left feet. She's new.'

Or, 'Lovely looking girl: not too top-heavy; dirty, dirty smile.'

I wasn't too sure if he was saying these things for my benefit or just thinking aloud. Either way, my microphone picked up his musings. In the early hours of the morning, I scurried back to Capital Radio in Euston Tower and handed in my tape. I got £40 for my shift.

Towards the end of my time in Cardiff I secured a two-week student placement at Moray Firth Radio in Inverness. I had never been this far north, but the station's studios were located on a hill overlooking the town on one side and, on the other, offered a stunning vista of the Kessock Bridge linking the Black Isle. That in itself was enough for me to fall in love with the place. In the six years since its launch, Moray Firth Radio had forged a strong relationship with its listeners and connected communities as far north as Wick and as far east as Fraserburgh.

I remember many news stories at the time dealing with the planned expansion of Inverness. Councillors debated plans for housing developments and retail parks and the possible environmental impact, especially on the famous dolphins basking off the coast. Dolphin-watching was, and is, a big thing in that part of Scotland, but I have to confess I always found them disappointing. You could stand for an hour at Chanonry Point – the spit of land favoured by dolphin devotees – and if they appeared at all, they would simply splash about in the distance. More tiresome were the supposed sightings of the Loch Ness Monster or the never-ending stream of charity groups passing through en route from Land's End to John O'Groats.

What I really enjoyed, oddly enough, was covering the meetings of the Highland Council. The constant friction between tradition and progress created a rich seam of stories as councillors battled over topics such as Gaelic road signs, sewage-treatment plants, Sunday opening hours and a stretch of road just east of Inverness that had been earmarked for the town's expansion and dubbed the 'Golden Mile'. I imagined its future as something akin to the Las Vegas Strip, but it's now home to a Tesco superstore and a multiplex cinema.

Our main competitor for news was BBC Radio Scotland, or more specifically, the opt-out service BBC Radio Highland. The BBC news team in Inverness seemed, to us, to be obsessed with crofters in the Western Isles. No press release from the Crofters Commission went unreported and, much to our delight, the BBC often missed stories on their own doorstep. On one very busy afternoon, alongside various council rows and road accidents, we led our bulletins with the story of how an RAF bomb – that should have been dropped on the training range at Tain – had gone astray and fallen on nearby farmland. My call to the local MP, Charles Kennedy, had prompted an immediate question in Parliament. Dropping bombs in the wrong place was a pretty big deal. That evening we tuned into Radio Highland to see if they had also picked up the story. Instead the BBC newsreader led on the resolution of a postal strike in the Western Isles, and the top line was: 'Everyone on the Isle of Lewis got their unemployment benefit cheques on time this morning.'

There was no mention of bombs. We were too surprised to laugh.

As I got to the end of my second week at Moray Firth Radio, the News Editor, Mike Hurry, pulled me aside and told me that he had been impressed with my efforts and that there was a reporter's job coming available at the end of the year. If I was interested – and duh, yes, I was – all I had to do was go with him to the pub and beat him in a game of pool. As recruitment processes went, this was an odd one, although I have to say that it might have been just as effective as all the pseudo-scientific 'competency-based' assessments that the BBC introduced.

Anyway, come six o'clock on Friday night, we trooped down to the Clachnaharry Bar, ordered beer and mutton stovies (with oatcakes) and slipped into the back room, where my Pool Table of Destiny awaited. I made a great play of chalking my cue because, to be honest, this was the only aspect of the game I knew I could handle without embarrassment. To say that I was beaten doesn't cover it. It was pure slapstick as I did everything apart from spear the green baize. There were balls everywhere. I considered it a triumph if I hit anything, even the overhead lighting strip.

At the end of the game, Mike commiserated and said it was a pity he wouldn't be working with me after all, but he wished me all the best for the future. Of course, before the end of the year, he called to offer me the job.

So, that's how I started my career. But my actual obsession with radio began when I was fourteen years old, living the life of a bedroom hermit in Easterhouse, the vast housing scheme on the outskirts of Glasgow. My big sister, Rose, had introduced me to Radio Clyde, because she was a fan of *Doctor Dick's Midnight Surgery*. Richard Park presented this mix of sixties music and phone-in competitions and was famous for flirting with female callers and suggesting that he might pop in to visit them on his way home. It all sounded much more daring than anything on the BBC.

When Rose got married and left home, I inherited her transistor radio set and explored the rest of the radio dial. I soon came across short-wave stations like BBC World Service, Radio Moscow, Radio Free Europe. I even entered a competition on a Radio Prague English-language music show, for which I was rewarded, some months later, with the arrival of a vinyl disc of Czech folk songs. Noticing the postmark, my Polish-born dad frowned at my dalliance with Soviet-controlled propaganda stations, so I scurried back to the safety of AM and FM and then I got in deep: I began writing short stories for an overnight show on Radio Clyde.

This was presented by Mike McLean and it was the era of 'needle time', which restricted the type and amount of commercial music that a disc jockey was allowed to play. Rather than squander the station's allowance in the pre-dawn hours, the overnight jocks had come up with innovative ways of filling the airtime with a lot more speech content than you would ever hear in daytime. Mike McLean invited his insomniac listeners to submit their own stories and poems from which he would choose four or five. These he would read aloud in the ultra-convenient hour between 4 a.m. and 5 a.m. My contributions were spoof detective tales featuring the exploits of cowardly investigator Nelson S. Pipsqueak. I used the pseudonym 'Jay Zed' for my scribblings. The style and dialogue were exaggeratedly Chandler-esque: if Nelson was being interrogated by a Mafia gangster then he would tell you that his 'Lips were flapping faster than a shutter on a stormy night', or that he was 'Spilling more beans than a cowboy with the shakes' ... that kind of thing.

The thrill for me as a teenage radio anorak was not just in hearing these stories broadcast to the nightshift workers of West Central Scotland, but in working to a weekly deadline to hand-deliver my submissions every Saturday. Once a week I would get the bus into town and make my way to Radio Clyde's studios in the city centre. As I climbed the stairs at Rankin House, I tried to eke out my moments lingering at the reception desk, hoping there would be a visitor or two in front of me so that I could spend a precious minute or so peering around, looking down corridors in the expectation of glimpsing one of the disc jockeys.

On one particular trek into town I saw the station's news reporter, Paul Cooney, wearing his red Radio Clyde jacket, hooking a backpack of complicated equipment over his shoulders as he emerged from his branded jeep. The idea of becoming a journalist had appealed to me ever since I'd seen the *Lou Grant* series on TV, in which Edward Asner played the grumpy editor of a newspaper and his team of young reporters was let loose on the streets to unearth stories about political corruption, gay rights and water pollution. Watching Paul Cooney set up his outside broadcast gear made me think for the first time about how I might combine journalism with radio.

Such sightings were rare, and on most Saturdays, I handed over my typewritten manuscript and left. This I did regularly for six months and then the unthinkable happened: Mike's show was axed. I was disappointed but happy to regain a normal sleep pattern. Then came a mysterious phone call: a woman's voice, soft and whispering; the kind of call I could have imagined from wartime, when resistance fighters in Occupied Europe had to be careful about what they said.

'Am I speaking to Jay Zed?'

'Yes.'

'The Jay Zed, who writes to Mike McLean?'

'Yes. Who is this?'

'Who I am doesn't matter. Some of us are launching a campaign to get Mike back on the air. Are you in?'

'Yes, but ...'

'Seven o'clock this Wednesday night. We're meeting at Central Station, at the bomb. Can you make it?'

'Depends on the bus. I mean, yes.'

The 'bomb' at Central Station was an old artillery shell that had been converted to collect cash donations for military charities. It had been a recognised rendezvous point in the city for decades. At seven o'clock on Wednesday I was among twenty or so regular listeners who gathered there waiting for our mysterious femme fatale to give us further instructions. To add to the cloak-and-dagger nature of the night, we all had to introduce ourselves to each other using the pseudonyms we had created when writing to the show. There was 'the Major', 'the Cornflake Freak', and so on. Then we had to reveal our actual identities. This took some time and then a blonde woman in her mid-thirties – was it she who had made the calls? – instructed us to take taxis to a pub in the East End. There we regrouped and began to discuss campaign tactics. I think it was after my third Irn-Bru that I heard one of our crowd talking about blowing up transmitters and another warmed to this idea so enthusiastically that he explained how he could get access to explosives and ammunition. He could get guns, he told us, and, if we wanted proof, he patted his coat pocket and told us that he was 'carrying'.

Nelson S. Pipsqueak himself would not have moved faster than me that night. I had survived sixteen years growing up in a Glasgow housing scheme without getting involved in gang culture or, in fact, in any nefarious activity beyond littering and overdue library books. I was not about to start my walk on the wild side that night just because of a stupid radio show.

My next involvement with Radio Clyde happened nine years later as I walked through the doors of the station's new studio complex in Clydebank (complete with indoor swimming pool), ready to begin my first day as a news reporter. In my eighteen months working for Mike Hurry at Moray Firth Radio, I had done enough to be noticed by the bosses at Clyde and make occasional appearances on the entire commercial radio network via Independent Radio News. I'd covered the collapse of the Ness Railway Bridge, the so-called Church Trial of Lord MacKay of Clashfern (he had incurred the displeasure of fellow Presbyterians by attending a Roman Catholic funeral), the hunt for a 'Casanova killer', who had fled from England to the Highlands seducing and murdering rich widows en route, and various stories about leaks, alleged leaks or safety fears at the Dounreay Nuclear Plant. I had become good friends with colleagues, such as Gary Robertson and Jackie O'Brien. It was hard to say goodbye, but now here I was, following in the footsteps of Paul Cooney, the gadgetry-festooned newsman I had spotted all those years ago – and I'd had a pay rise too.

When I told my dad that I was now earning £16,000 a year, he looked at me as if I'd announced I'd just won the pools. Compared to my salary at Moray Firth Radio, it felt that way.

Dad, who had been living alone since Mum had died and I'd gone off to Wales, was looking forward to me being closer to home, although my plan to save money by moving back into my old bedroom for a while lasted exactly one week. I had quickly regressed to the point where I felt guilty when he asked me why I had come in late and nauseous when he handed me his signature dish of blackened sausages, lard and eggs (memorably described by my appalled sister-in-law as looking like 'a monkey's abortion'). I realised I needed a place of my own and I rented a one-bedroom cottage by Loch Lomond, just a twenty-minute drive from the studios.

The Clyde newsroom had two blocks of desks pushed together to form long tables. Stories were typed on paper, with three carbon sheets attached. Each reporter was assigned a locker to store their Sony or Marantz cassette recorder and microphone. We were given a thick folder covering health and safety rules, which included instructions on how to approach the station's 'Eye in the Sky' traffic helicopter. Above the lockers was a bank of thick GPO telephone directories – a book for every part of Britain.

There was some discussion about my name. People were curious about my Polish origins and in hearing how my father, a sailor with the Polish Free Navy, had arrived in Glasgow during World War II and remained to marry my mother in peacetime. But there was uncertainty as to whether 'Jeff Zycinski' was a name that would sound right on the airwaves and probably more of a worry whether the disc jockeys would be able to pronounce it. There was even talk of giving me a new stage name and I recall that 'Jeff Scotland' was one of the suggestions. I solved the problem by spelling my name phonetically on any written news cues and doing the same for the programme presenters if I was on duty as a bulletin reader: Jeff Ziz-in-ski.

All new reporters were sent to a voice coach and given exercises to stretch the lips and improve diction. These involved mouthing nonsense phrases such as 'Bibbity Babbity' over and over again. I was told off for referring to the Queen's sister in the Glaswegian style, as Princess *Mag-ret*, and pronouncing the name of the French tennis player Guy Forget as if he were an amnesiac on Bonfire Night. Scottish people, our coach told us, have a tendency to speak so fast that they would neglect to sound out the end of words. The solution was simple: slow down and think about the meaning of each word in the script. When Radio Clyde split into two services – Clyde 1, for younger listeners, and Clyde 2 for the heartland – we had to choose different stories for each target audience and adapt our writing and delivery style for each station. David Johnstone, a formidable news editor at Radio Forth, once joked that the breakfast news on Clyde 2 was read so slowly that he had enough time between sentences to nip down to the shops and read the stories in the newspapers.

All the same, when I was first with a story, when I knew listeners would be leaning forward to hear what I was saying, there was something thrilling about sitting in the studio, watching the second hand of the clock tick towards the top of the hour, seeing the red light and hearing the DJ announce my name. The news sting fired and I told the world – or at the least the West of Scotland – something they didn't already know, and something that someone else might not want told. News.

Those early days in the Clyde newsroom were fast-paced, fun and exactly how I had imagined life for a reporter in such a big city; a city renowned for its gritty, violent image. But this was the 1990s and, as the soot-blackened tenement blocks were being sand-blasted back to gleaming red and blonde sandstone, the people who lived in them were now embracing the idea that Glasgow was a true European Capital of Culture: Pavarotti turned up to sing for a new generation of opera fans and Frank Sinatra played Ibrox stadium.

Yet the undercurrent of menace was never far away. Mafia-style warfare erupted again in the East End and our hourly bulletins described the murders of gangland bosses and the deaths, or killings, of low-level drug dealers and addicts. I found myself climbing tenement stairs to interview shocked neighbours or grieving mothers.

Every journalist can tell tales about stories they covered, or the famous names they met. When the Prime Minister, Margaret Thatcher, came to open the St Enoch Shopping Centre, I was at the front of the press pack, behind a guard rail, shoving my microphone towards her and asking question after question about the previous day's poll tax riots in London and the fortunes of the Conservative Party in Scotland. Determined that she would have the last word, she kept returning to my microphone to offer another platitude about the welcome she was receiving in Scotland. I ended up with a ten-minute interview. When her minders finally persuaded her to move on, the gaggle of reporters congratulated me on my bravery and pleaded with me to press 'playback' on my tape machine so that they could grab quotes for their own articles. I obliged. I'm a sucker for flattery.

Slow news days were when you really earned your crust, and where you got the chance to use all you had learned about keeping a good contacts book and calling around to chase up leads. On my days off I would pursue tip-offs about vigilante groups tackling drug dealers in Balloch. I won a New York Festival award for a spooky scoop about a ghost cooking roast beef at Stirling Castle. I kept notes about things I'd seen in shop windows or on library noticeboards. If nothing else was doing, that daft story about clog dancers in Coatbridge could fill a good half-minute.

Alas, the slow days could also skew your moral compass. One very quiet Christmas I was working a solo backshift when nothing was stirring, not even a mouse infestation in the Gorbals. Then the telex machine started stuttering out some copy about an attempted murder in Surrey, but 'Joy to the World!' I cried, when it emerged the victim was from Fife. Not that I wished anyone from Fife anything less than a long and fruitful life, but a story with a Scottish angle was a godsend on a quiet day

There was real pride in beating the BBC to a story and the Clyde mobile news van – known internally as 'the Death Mobile' – allowed us a fast turnaround in sending copy and audio back to the studios in Clydebank. That vehicle was a thing to be feared. It was a Mitsubishi van with a bolted-on telescopic mast, which made the whole thing top-heavy, so I said a small prayer every time we took a curve at more than 20 mph. Luckily, the hairdryer engine made it impossible to get up any speed, but the lack of oomph also made it a struggle to climb the slightest of gradients. On too many assignments I found myself, red-faced at the wheel of that van, grinding out of the Clyde Tunnel in first gear, while trying to ignore a tailback of cars and frustrated drivers behind me.

We would meet BBC news reporters at press conferences. The Beeb never seemed to be short-staffed. Whereas one of their reporters would cover the conference for radio, another would arrive with his sound engineer and TV cameraman. Occasionally another BBC bod would turn up for the Gaelic angle and, if it was a story worthy of UK interest, a network crew would arrive to do it all for London. We suspected that for these lucky sods from the BBC, this one story might occupy them all day, whereas it was normal for a commercial radio reporter to cover four or five jobs in a shift, shuttling from one location to another and reporting back to base on the Death Mobile's walkie-talkie.

When working for Clyde, I had one encounter with the Controller of BBC Scotland, John McCormick, which, for the duration of my career there, I always feared he might remember. The occasion was the unveiling of the BBC's *Extending Choice* document – the masterplan on how the Corporation would survive and be given another Royal Charter by offering programmes that were distinctive from commercial television and radio. Clyde's ultimate boss and CEO, James Gordon, had asked if a reporter could nip up to BBC Scotland's HQ at Queen Margaret Drive and get him a copy of the document. The Duty News Editor, Clare McCarren, thought it would be a pity to do that and not

27

come back with a story. I attended the conference which, to be honest, was always going to be of more interest to people in the industry than to the general public. The published document had lots of details about production quotas for the independent sector and, by including network radio in those quotas, the BBC hoped to stave off Tory Government calls for Radio 1 and Radio 2 to be privatised.

This was dull stuff for the average viewer or listener, but still, I asked if I might record an interview with the Controller. This request seemed to surprise the Press Office staff and I was left killing time in a conference room while, every now and then, an assistant would pop her head around the door, probably hoping I had given up. Eventually John McCormick invited me in to his deep-pile carpeted office and we started recording. He gave me the corporate line about quality and distinctiveness being more important than large viewing figures. By the time I made it back to the Death Mobile I had the top line written in my head: 'The BBC is waving the white flag in the battle for audiences'.

It was very cheeky – and I'm told the sales team upstairs at Radio Clyde used it with clients when trying to sell advertising.

The management style at Clyde was … well, *robust*. It was a culture in which I learned a lot because even small mistakes were quickly highlighted and no one wanted to make the same blunder twice. That same culture also instilled fear and nervousness and could sap a person's self-confidence. If a colleague left to take up a new job elsewhere, the Head of News and Current Affairs would appear in the newsroom and announce that there must be something wrong with the rest of us because we were still there; there was a queue of people waiting to take our jobs, he would tell us, just in case we got any ideas that we might be valued.

The macho attitude in the newsroom might have been a hangover from the days when the original staff had been recruited from the ranks of Scottish newspapers. Perhaps the scale of Radio Clyde's success had tipped some managers over the edge from pride to arrogance. There was certainly a lot to be proud of: Clyde at that time had a market share that was bigger than all of the BBC stations put together. In the days before national commercial stations were launched, they had no radio competitors for advertising revenue. One of the first community stations, East End Radio, spluttered on to the airwaves for a few months, but couldn't make a dent in the loyalty of Clyde's audience, nor compete with the quality of its programmes. It soon folded.

The individual reporters on our team were hard-working and mutually supportive. I worked alongside people like Mark Leishman, who kept quiet about the fact he was the grandson of Lord Reith, the BBC's first Director General. Richard Gordon had joined from Northsound Radio in Aberdeen, but his real passion was football and he left to become the main presenter of *Sportsound* on Radio Scotland. Ken Mitchell's voice is now familiar to many as a television announcer at BBC Scotland. Clare Dean joined STV and then became a university lecturer. Audrey Munro went to work for a radio station in Switzerland. It was a good bunch of people, but this was a 24/7 news service and the staggered shift patterns meant there were few opportunities for us all to be in one place at one time or to socialise together.

Also, because we often had to work well beyond our official stopping time, it was difficult to make arrangements with friends outside of work and be sure of keeping a date. Nevertheless, as a young, single man in his twenties, I was on the lookout for romance and found it with Anne, a research scientist working at the University of Glasgow. At the time she was being funded to test different strains of peas and determine which might survive in ultra-saline conditions, such as a desert. On my days off I would visit her in her lab and it was refreshing to be in the company of people other than newshounds or radio freaks. It did amuse me that these dedicated scientists often seemed very far removed from the outside world. Not to be cruel, but I suspect some might have struggled to pass one of those capacity tests they gave in hospital when someone was old or concussed: you know, where they ask you to say what day of the week it is or to name the current Prime Minister. Likewise, when Anne met my journalist friends, she was less than enchanted by their all-consuming obsession with the media.

My relationship with Anne was the cause of a near bust-up with my newsroom editor. One night, having been due to leave work at 5 p.m., I was still hammering out stories an hour later and feeling more resentful by the minute. Finally, I exploded and ranted that tonight of all nights I needed to get out of the 'bloody office!'

There was a sudden hush in the office and all eyes turned in my direction. This kind of outburst was unthinkable. Had mild-mannered Jeff lost his mind? The editor was taken aback. 'What's so special about tonight?' he demanded to know.

'Because tonight I'm asking Anne to marry me.'

Happily, he let me get my coat … and more happily, Anne said 'yes'.

3.

MONEY FOR OLD ROPE

It was a cruel joke – one that was eventually to bite me on the bum – and I really shouldn't have been trying to outwit my own Best Man, but the opportunity was too good to miss. Among our hundred or so wedding guests were at least half a dozen of my newsroom colleagues from Radio Clyde. Gary, on the other hand, was one of our bitter rivals so, as I thanked him for his speech, I noted, 'Some of you may already know that Gary Robertson works as a producer at BBC Radio Scotland, so this is one of the biggest audiences he's had in a very long time.'

Cue the cheers and guffaws from the Clyde tables. Anyone who worked in commercial radio would have told you of the delight they felt when tiny David got a chance to throw rocks at this Goliath of broadcasting. It became almost obligatory to sneer at the Beeb's self-importance, pomposity and apparent cavalier approach to spending licence-payers' money. Michael Grade, when running Channel 4, had talked about the BBC wallowing in Jacuzzis of cash. This might have seemed preferable to a swimming pool, but if you didn't work there – or worse, had tried and failed to get a job there – then it was the done thing to say you *never* wanted to work there.

'You need to come and work here,' Gary had told me just a few days after Anne and I returned from our honeymoon in New England. 'It's money for old rope.'

Gary and I had become friends when working in Inverness. When I left to go to Radio Clyde in Glasgow, Gary joined the BBC in Dumfries as an assistant producer with Radio Solway. His boss there had been amazed that Gary had so many skills; skills that anyone in commercial radio just took for granted. This had prompted Gary's 'money for old rope' analysis. He himself had made quick work of his climb up the greasy pole and had moved to be a news producer in Glasgow. Now he was telling me about a producer vacancy at the BBC's Inverness office and urging me to apply. This required a discussion with Anne. Her research had continued at Glasgow University, but she was becoming disillusioned because the balance of her work was moving away from actual science and she was spending more and more time making grant applications. This was the period when lots of Government funding was being directed to the Human Genome Project, and her recent applications had been turned down.

She, like me, was in the mood for a change and as we were now married it would be no bad thing to get a grown-up job so that we had the financial security needed to start a family. Everyone said a job at the BBC was a 'job for life'.

The urban legend had it that the only way you could ever be sacked from the BBC was if they found out you hadn't paid for your TV licence. This was almost true, but, as I discovered in later years, that job security had less to do with the licence-fee issue and more to do with the reluctance of BBC managers and personnel officers to confront unions.

With Anne's support, I applied for the Inverness job. A few weeks later, wearing a crisp white shirt and monochrome tie, I was about to go before one of the BBC's infamous interview 'boards' and try to persuade the panel of interrogators that I was the man for the job. I would do this in the most unusual way – by telling them that I wasn't.

James Boyle ran Radio Scotland at the time and Scottish newspapers such as *The Herald* and *The Scotsman* had been giving him plenty of coverage, because his schedule changes were causing quite a stir with listeners. They were also creating a lot of nervousness among the on-air talent as they came to realise that James' vision of quality broadcasting was blind to the delights of cheeky-chappie disc jockeys chatting inanely about their daily horoscopes.

I didn't realise it at the time, but James was a rare breed at the BBC: he was prepared to own hard decisions, act quickly and live with the flak. He also had a keen ear for what made a good broadcaster and had just persuaded Eddie Mair to give up co-presenting the morning news programme – *Good Morning Scotland* – and host his own mid-morning show, called *Eddie Mair Live*. Not everyone was a fan and it was indicative of the times that some of the criticism focused on Eddie's sexuality rather than his obvious skill and flair as a broadcaster, but listeners soon warmed to Eddie's own brand of satirical humour and irreverent features. Dickens' classic *A Tale of Two Cities* was being serialised as a sentence a day … and lawyers invited on air were accompanied by the sound effect of a cash register for every question they answered. There was also a plan to deal with listeners who complained about blasphemous language: they were to be invited on air and then, recalling the fate of Christians at the Coliseum, faded out to the sound of a roaring lion. I don't think that idea ever made it to the airwaves, but Eddie's show, more than anything, demonstrated that Radio Scotland was changing and most people in the industry knew the change was long overdue.

As the national BBC station for Scotland, it was often criticised for trying to be all things to all people. A fairer assessment is that it was fulfilling the remit of a full-service public broadcaster by offering news, sport, music, drama, arts coverage, religion, and so on and so on. People might listen for Scottish news and then switch off. Or they might tune in only for the sport coverage at weekends … or a comedy show like *Naked Radio*. But when it came to disc-based entertainment, it was hard to beat local commercial radio, or the then powerhouse that was Radio 1. Radio Scotland DJs tried their best to sound like they were *down with the kids*, but record request shows often had calls from women named 'Bunty', asking that the next song be dedicated to their home help or health visitor.

Not that any of these things were discussed at my job interview. Instead, James seized on that tiny section at the foot of my application form where I had listed 'movies and music' as my interests and hobbies. I mean, no one ever asks about those things anyway, do they?

'So what music were you listening to in the car on the way here?' James asked.

This might have been the point at which I was supposed to mention a particular radio programme or, at the very least, a highbrow piece of orchestral music. Instead I told him I had an old Sinatra cassette warbling away from the one good speaker in my old Audi 80. There then ensued a discussion that almost became an argument about the kind of music and orchestrations that best suited Ol' Blue Eyes. I name-dropped Cole Porter, and James came back with Nelson Riddle. We then moved on to movies. I talked about Hitchcock and James asked for an analysis of *Marnie*. I talked about the dream sequences and whether the phoney look of the sets had been intentional or a result of budget restraints. It seemed like we were on the verge of fisticuffs with this nonsense when we were interrupted by Maggie Cunningham. (Maggie was the Campus Editor in charge of all the Gaelic and English-language output in Inverness. If I got the job, she would be my boss.) She asked if she could 'Bring you men back down to earth', and brandished the letter which I had submitted with my form.

'You've written here,' she said, 'that you're *not* actually capable of doing this job; the job you've applied for. I don't understand.'

Now, hang on, let me explain this. You see, when Gary had told me about this job being up for grabs in Inverness, he'd described it as a 'producer' post. As an outsider, unfamiliar with the management hierarchy in the BBC, I had yet to find out that a producer was broadly equivalent to reporter level in commercial radio. A Senior Producer was like a Senior Reporter, which is the level I had reached at Clyde. The vacant post in Inverness, it turned out, was actually for an executive producer. This seemed to me to be up there with the gods and so, along with my pro-forma application, I had written a note saying that I thought it unlikely I could make the leap from a journalistic position in commercial radio to an executive position at the BBC. I asked, however, if they would interview me in the hope that they might consider me for some future vacancy that might arise. You could call this honesty, stupidity or just wasting everyone's time. It certainly struck Maggie as odd and I wasn't surprised when, after returning home to describe the interview to Anne, I got a call from Carol in the Personnel Office telling me that I had been unsuccessful in my application.

'But,' she added, 'is there any way you could pop back in this afternoon? There's something else we want to talk to you about.'

'Of course,' I said, moving quickly through mature disappointment to renewed enthusiasm. 'When do you want me to come back?'

'In about half an hour?'

'No problem. On my way.'

The crisp white shirt I had worn that morning was now lying balled up in the laundry basket and the tie was somewhere down the back of the sofa. I had torn them off and slipped into an old t-shirt as soon as I got home. I told Anne what had been said on the phone. She went for the ironing board, I dived behind the sofa and thirty minutes later I was being offered a job as BBC Radio Scotland's Senior Producer in Selkirk.

Personally, I attribute my success to that shirt and tie. Back home, Anne was delighted. We opened a bottle of room-temperature Hirondelle white wine and then got the AA Road Atlas out of the car.

Selkirk was not, as we had feared, off the edge of the world. It's a two-hour drive from Glasgow and, as you hit the Scottish Borders, you find yourself in some of the most glorious scenery that Scotland has to offer. The rolling hills beside the Tweed are as picturesque as anything you can see in, say, Highland Perthshire. When Anne and I went on our first house-hunting mission, we were both astounded and delighted by what we encountered around the border towns of Galashiels, Jedburgh, Hawick, Melrose and Kelso. Selkirk, on the other hand, was like many of the old mill towns: it had seen better days. All the Border towns had suffered from the closure of the railway link in the 1960s. It has since been re-opened and the trains are running again, but at that time, in the mid-1990s, it was as if this part of Scotland had been left in a curious time warp.

It was less than an hour's drive up the A7 to Edinburgh, but it felt like we skipped decades between locations. Shops in Selkirk, for example, still adhered to an early closing day. In fact, it had three of them, including Saturdays. Some of the local pubs refused to serve women at the bar; others were more progressive and would allow female customers to buy beer, but only in half-pint glasses. The big events in these towns were the Common Ridings, an annual colourful pageant that honoured the traditional marking of the boundaries by horseback riders. Each of the towns had their own riding event and there was much rivalry, especially between Selkirk and Galashiels – or 'Gala', as it's known locally. Once, when shopping at the local Presto in Selkirk, the checkout assistant had remarked on the rainy weather and added, smiling, 'It's the Gala Common Riding today.' The thought of her nearby neighbours having a washout event had brightened her own day considerably.

We found a house to rent, but Radio Clyde insisted on holding me to the full three months of my contractual notice period, so I couldn't start with the BBC until the first day of November. In the meantime, I was sent all the necessary paperwork from Personnel, which included details of my entitlement to luncheon vouchers and how I could apply for discounted 'country membership' of the BBC Club.

Our semi-detached, two-bedroom home in Ladylands Terrace was a step up from the modern tenement flat we had shared in Glasgow. As we settled in, I got the chance to listen to the output from Radio Scotland and, in particular, the local opt-out programmes that came from the Selkirk studios. They gave me a lot to think about. The traditional role of the senior producer in Selkirk had been to manage the output of Radio Tweed. The snag here was that James Boyle, in his efforts to channel as much cash as possible into programmes for the main Radio Scotland service, had closed Radio Tweed, alongside its counterparts in Dumfries (Radio Solway), Inverness (Radio Highland) and Aberdeen (Radio Aberdeen).

There had been much bitterness about this and angry protests at public meetings. But James had stuck to his guns. Those local stations would now operate as satellite production centres, providing opt-out news and sport bulletins four times a day (not at weekends, public holidays or during the festive season). I was particularly interested in the quality of those bulletins and thought they were lagging well behind what could be heard on the new commercial station, Radio Borders.

At this stage, just a few days before I took up my post and before I had met anyone in the Selkirk office, I tried to imagine how I might approach the job. First, I had to unravel BBC Scotland's complicated management structure and work out who reported to whom in the chain of command. My line manager, it turned out, was the Campus Editor in Edinburgh, Allan Jack. He reported through the Managing Editor for Radio, Caroline Adam. She in turn reported to James Boyle. He reported to the Controller of BBC Scotland, John McCormick. John reported to the then Head of Nations and Regions, Mark Thompson, and he reported to the Director General (DG), John Birt. Alongside this, there was a whole oversight structure in the form of a Board of Governors in London, a National Governor for Scotland and an Audience Council for Scotland. The latter comprised 'ordinary members of the public' charged with representing the interests of viewers and listeners.

So where did BBC News fit in to this? Not at all, as it turns out, because News was – and is – a separate division that reports up through a different command chain through the Deputy Director General and then to the DG. So, any thoughts I had about reading the riot act to the Selkirk newsroom were negated by the fact that, as Senior Producer, I had no responsibility for news. Also, since the demise of Radio Tweed, I had no actual output to oversee. So even before I walked through the door of the Council Office on the High Street and up the steep staircase to the offices leased by BBC Scotland, I began to wonder if the job I had been given existed. And if it existed, was it needed?

How someone imagines things will be and how things are, are always two different things. Walking into the BBC's Selkirk office I was greeted by Clare, the part-time receptionist who introduced me to Ninian Reid, an affable newsman, who had cut his teeth in the heady days of the Glasgow newspaper wars. Now he was the main Network Reporter for BBC Scotland, which meant he didn't – or shouldn't – have to trouble himself with trifling local stories. He had people to do that for him: a team of three reporters crammed into a tiny newsroom adjacent to the kitchen.

I, on the other hand, was shown into a sizeable office, dominated by a huge desk set against a bay window that looked out on the High Street. Below was the statue of Mungo Park, famed for his explorations in Africa in the eighteenth and nineteenth centuries. Across the street was that Presto mini-mart. The drawers of the desk were empty but for several Kit Kat biscuits. Clare explained that my predecessor had had a fondness for Kit Kats and coffee. 'And the guy before him was obsessed with flags.'

'Flags?'

'Yes, he wanted a wall-mounted flagpole outside the building so that he could fly the BBC flag here in the Borders.'

'Why?'

'So that he could mark royal birthdays and deaths. He wrote lots of letters to London about it but had no joy.'

'Who did he write to?'

'I'm not sure. There might be a Head of Flags.'

'Really? I suppose it's possible.'

So, chocolate biscuits and flags. But at least those guys had had a local radio station to run. As I sat at my desk, alone in my big office, listening to the chatter coming from the newsroom (which wasn't my responsibility), I thought about how busy things would have been at Clyde. Money for old rope was all very well, but the hours would drag if all I had to do was count the knots.

I called my boss in Edinburgh. His advice was enigmatic and unhelpful. 'Just don't go native,' he told me.

'What does that mean?'

'You know … don't cover jumble sales and the like.'

'I won't.'

I eked out the rest of that first day familiarising myself with the radio studio and the control desk. In the technical cupboard I found some reel-to-reel tape recorders alongside a Sony Walkman Professional cassette recorder. I discovered the station had two pool cars in the back car park, but only Ninian had a driving licence and he had been issued with his own News car. It struck me as odd that the other reporters would think nothing of catching a bus if they wanted to cover a council meeting or a police press conference in a neighbouring town.

Clare explained the petty-cash system and told me that the cleaner had been complaining about the faulty vacuum cleaner. I had a quick look at the old Electrolux cylinder machine, with its buckled hoses patched together with duct tape, and declared it a write-off. My first major decision for the British Broadcasting Corporation, therefore, was to authorise Clare to spend some of the petty cash on a new Hoover. I didn't clear this decision with the Head of Suction or anyone in Edinburgh, Glasgow or London.

What's the worst that could happen? I thought, and that was to be my motto for the next twenty-five years.

4.

BLOKES ON BLOCKS

The statue of Mungo Park out there on the High Street gave me my first idea for a series of programmes that I could pitch to James Boyle. Selkirk-born Park was an explorer and missionary credited with being the first Westerner to have travelled to the hitherto undiscovered reaches of the Niger River in West Africa. His effigy stood on a plinth at the foot of which were four black slaves, or bearers. All in all, it gave the impression of a great man, a true Scottish hero, and one who still commanded respect here and abroad. Yet when I began to scratch the surface of Mungo Park's story, all was not as it seemed. His expeditions did not all go well: many of those bearers died; he himself died on his last adventure; and, of course, the idea of white Europeans 'discovering' parts of Africa is now a bit suspect. I suggested to James Boyle that there might be a short series in which we looked again at the figures

– the bulk of them men – that we found carved in marble or bronze around our towns and cities. I suggested it be called *Blokes on Blocks*. Other historical figures in the series included the Duke of Sutherland, the man blamed for the Highland Clearances, whereas Sandy Semenoff's bust of Pat Lally, a controversial council leader in Glasgow, gave the series a contemporary edge.

James liked the programmes and I began to flood him with other ideas. He commissioned a series on famous hoaxes (*Waiting for Mermaids*), one on newspaper scoops (*Front Page Splash*), and another on women in sport (*Big Girls, No Blouses*). I began to recruit and train a small group of freelancers who could be called upon to make programme pieces for Radio Scotland's magazine shows. Among them was a young woman called Lisa Summers, who demonstrated her dedication by driving down from Edinburgh each day to pick up the odd bit of work and, as she put it, bring us news of the modern world fifty miles to the north. She also brought her fun and energy to the Selkirk office, organising team-bonding nights at events such as a curling competition (the icy kind, not hair-dressing) and a tarot card reading at a local hotel.

The trick, I discovered, was to keep feeding the schedule and I developed a simple formula: at least one episode in each series of programmes would have a local Borders angle, thus justifying my position in Selkirk; the others would have appeal across Scotland and beyond. The local story also gave me a reason to build contacts with the local press, so that we would get coverage in *The Southern Reporter* and *The Border Telegraph*. This seemed to me to be important given that there was still a lot of grumbling about the demise of Radio Tweed.

Not knowing that Radio Scotland's publicity activity was supposed to be handled – or at least approved – by the Press Office in Glasgow, I forged friendships with local newspaper reporters. As I saw it, we were BBC Radio Scotland in the Borders and my job – or the job I was trying to create for myself – was to be the champion for all things Beeb in this part of Scotland. So, when James Boyle's shake-up of the Radio Scotland schedule saw him collecting the UK Station of the Year prize at the prestigious Sony Radio Academy Awards, I let it be known to the local press that we, in Selkirk, were sharing in the celebrations. That prompted a few valuable paragraphs about champagne corks being popped.

Oddly though, there didn't seem to be similar efforts to trumpet this big win in the Glasgow or Edinburgh papers and that was another thing that I noticed was different about the BBC compared to commercial radio: success and failure were treated as equal impostors. So, when the newspaper cuttings were sent around the various managers' offices it looked as if the only person taking credit for the Sony glory was that wee team in the Borders, led by a man who was just in the door and couldn't have had anything to do with the programmes that had secured the win.

Seeing myself as an ambassador for the BBC also meant I had to take an interest in a certain yellow bear. Pudsey, the one-eyed teddy, was the mascot for BBC Children in Need, the Corporation's official charity. In the Borders, a stalwart supporter had been an accordionist and tutor called Bill Sharp, whose orchestra of young box players had performed a concert every November to raise cash for Pudsey. I discovered it was my job to go through to the concert at the Tait Hall in Kelso and make an onstage appearance at the end of the show. I would thank Bill, the audience and, of course, the young players who had done so much for the charity.

As I waited in the wings someone – I know not who – whispered in my ear, 'I hope you know the words.'

Before I could turn and ask what this meant, the show's host, Bill Torrance, invited me on stage and handed me a microphone. I blurted my spiel, provoked the audience into a round of applause and got a minor laugh when I handed Bill Sharp a bottle of brandy, with some remarks about this being payback for having warmed our hearts. All done and dusted. Or so I thought, until Bill Torrance addressed the audience with the announcement:

'And now Jeff will lead us all in his rendition of "We're no awa' tae bide awa'"'.'

What?

More applause. I heard the accordions revving up behind me. It was a menacing sound.

Now, you've probably heard the song 'We're no awa' tae bide awa" and you might, like me, know the first line, or even the second. Even supposing I thought I could carry a tune, what would happen when I reached that third line? Should I make up some new words on the hoof? Should I feign a fainting spell? Perhaps I could point to the back of the theatre and shout 'Fire! Fire!'

'Oh, we're no awa' tae bide awa' ...'

Going well so far.

'And we're no awa' tae leave ye ...'

And then I even remembered the next bit: 'We're no awa' tae bide awa', we'll aye come back and see ye ...'

Now I was running on empty.

And then I had a brainwave – I needed to blame the audience.

As the accordions billowed out for the next verse I pointed the microphone at the crowd and shouted, 'Come on! You lot can do better than that!'

And they carried the day with me clapping encouragement, nodding and smiling to the young musicians behind me as I walked backwards off the stage to leave the real stars of the show to bask in the limelight.

Anne, who had been in the front row enjoying every second of my embarrassment, caught up with me afterwards.

'I think you got away with that,' she said.

'Let's get in the car,' I told her. 'They might demand an encore.'

My next new experience at the BBC was a strike: the first of many industrial disputes I was to witness in the ensuing years, always accompanied by the phrase, 'Morale in the newsroom is at rock bottom.' In Selkirk the news team didn't show up for work and so there were no local bulletins that day. I had gone into the office to deal with any complaints from listeners. There were none. The next day I got a call from James Boyle, who was in teasing mood.

'Jeff, after yesterday's strike, we decided to victimise random employees and your name came out of the hat.'

I was about to protest when he continued.

'The boss is getting a group together to launch a *Programme Strategy Review* on the back of *Extending Choice*. I've put your name forward for that. There's a meeting in Glasgow at the end of the week. There are papers to read before the meeting, so I've arranged for the

Controller's driver to bring them to you this afternoon. Enjoy!'

There was a lot to take in here. Firstly, my only knowledge of *Extending Choice* came from my encounter with John McCormick. Would he be at the meeting? Secondly, the Controller of BBC Scotland had a driver? Thirdly, this was all so important that these papers had to be sent to me this afternoon?

I think that was the first time I began to feel less like a forgotten employee in a BBC backwater and instead, part of something bigger; part of the organisation. A couple of hours later, a dark-suited chauffeur appeared at the Selkirk reception desk asking for me and saying that he had to deliver the package of papers directly into my hands. It was like something from a spy novel. I sympathised with the driver for his four-hour round trip, took the bundle of graphs and charts from him and was determined that I would prove myself up to the task. These papers would not fall into the wrong hands, and if rivals from, say, ITV tried to get information from me, I would defy every torture they could devise, up to and including being forced to watch old episodes of *Highway* with Sir Harry Secombe.

On close inspection, however, the information in my hands was hardly worthy of the BBC's 'Confidential – Not for Wider Distribution' stamp. They contained the kind of charts and graphs you would have found in most broadcast industry magazines at the time. *Extending Choice*, as an initiative, boiled down to this; the BBC should offer programmes and services that weren't being provided by other broadcasters so that listeners and viewers had … well … more choice. That's my own executive summary.

The actual documents in my hand ran to several pages and about 5,000 words. Worse was to come when I turned up for the meeting in Glasgow and two strategists from London began their PowerPoint presentation. Ten minutes in and they were still on the second slide. My attention wandered to some small figures at the corner of their slide: 2/79. No! Could this be? We were on the second of seventy-nine slides and already ten minutes had expired. I started to doodle some sums in my notebook. Given that the first slide was just a title sheet, we had just spent nine minutes on the second slide. There were seventy-seven slides to go:

$$77 \times 9 = ... \text{ let me see } ... 693 \text{ minutes.}$$

Suddenly the door of the conference room opened and in walked the sharp-suited and debonair figure of John McCormick, Controller of BBC Scotland. John's first words boomed out, silencing the strategists and sending the blood draining from my face.

'Is Jeff Zycinski in the room?'

This felt so much like the headmaster intervening at a school assembly that I found myself raising a hand. All eyes turned to me.

'Yes, he is. I mean, I'm him. It's me.'

John pointed a finger and walked towards me smiling, his own hand outstretched.

'I want to shake your hand,' he said. 'That press coverage you've been getting for us in the Borders is terrific, and it's so important.'

I was taken aback but muttered a modest, 'Thank you'.

Now, I have been to literally hundreds of BBC meetings in my career, but I've never forgotten the impact of that encounter with John. I worked away doing my job, hoping it was being appreciated or at least hoping I wasn't getting it too badly wrong. Then to have a boss single me out for praise ... well, I could take that to the bank.

I might not make much of it in front of my colleagues because it wasn't the done thing to look too chuffed, but I took the praise home, shared it with my wife and used it to top up my inner reservoir of self-confidence. It was a real lesson in good management and the power of a simple bit of positive feedback – not something I was used to at Radio Clyde.

I was invited to those Glasgow meetings every couple of weeks and did my best to chuck in my tuppence-worth about the future of broadcasting. As well as dropping in on Dad on the way home, I also got to catch up with what was happening with the rest of Radio Scotland. The *Eddie Mair Live* show was still going strong, but there were rumours that Eddie himself was being courted by the soon-to-be-launched BBC 5 Live.

His production team had commissioned me to make and present the occasional programme piece for the show and I would track down offbeat stories, such as the two women – both lifelong Ken Dodd fans – who spent their weekends tracking down Dodd and Diddy Men memorabilia. I had persisted with my habit of spelling my name phonetically in scripts, but Eddie always introduced me as 'Jeff Zycinski, spelled *Zycinski*'.

Meanwhile, in Edinburgh, preparations were underway for the Edinburgh Festivals. The BBC's approach to this event – the world's biggest arts festival – had always mystified me. The radio and television teams would arrive from all corners to offer their own take on this annual feast of music, comedy, drama, dance, mime and experimental juggling, but you might be hard-pressed to appreciate the scale of the BBC's interest, because each team took up residence in a different venue. So, BBC Radio Scotland would mount shows from their own studios in Queen Street; Radio 4 would be up at the Pleasance; Radio 3 would be at the Queen's Hall; and so on. Meanwhile, a station like Virgin Radio would construct a massive marquee atop Waverley train station and, despite limited amount of actual programming, would give the impression that, during August, they owned Edinburgh. I couldn't help wondering why the BBC didn't pool its resources and make a big splash in one single venue.

But I was still wet behind the ears and naive to the internal politics of the situation. I didn't realise then that getting Radio 4 to talk to Radio 2 was slightly more difficult than creating dialogue between Israelis and Palestinians in the Middle East. Nevertheless, Edinburgh in August gave me my first chance to make programmes away from Selkirk. Jane Fowler, then in charge of Arts Programming for Radio Scotland, asked me to journey up the A7 and work on her *Centre Stage* series of short lunchtime documentaries that would run each weekday on Radio Scotland during the festivals.

She asked me if I would like to tackle the subject of gay and lesbian theatre, which she had identified as being a key theme of that year: there was much talk about the economic impact of 'the pink pound and the lavender dollar'. I grabbed my new digital recorder and dashed around the city recording interviews and persuading actors to perform short (copyright-free) excerpts of their plays. Back in the Queen

Street office, I wrote my script, chose some music and booked some time in a studio to mix the whole thing. It was all done and dusted by the following morning and I presented Jane with the completed programme.

'What's this?' she asked,

'It's the programme. All done. Have a listen.'

Jane's puzzlement became clear when she explained that most producers would take at least a week to complete one of these short features. My days at Radio Clyde had made me work to a self-imposed deadline. I began to doubt myself. Maybe an arts feature needed more pondering time than I had allowed? Perhaps I should have ruminated over a glass of absinthe? Or maybe not, as Jane and I were delighted when my 'pink pound' edition of *Centre Stage* got a glowing review in the weekend newspapers.

I was heading back to Selkirk when I got a call asking if I could do a couple of weeks with Eddie Mair's *Live* team. By then, news of Eddie's departure had been confirmed and I would be there for his last week on Radio Scotland and the bedding in of a new format presented by Karen Clarke.

This was all fun for me, but by the time I did get back to Selkirk, Anne was finding small town life a little claustrophobic. We had now bought the house we had been renting in Ladylands Terrace and were preparing to settle there for another year or two, but with no children yet, it was difficult to make friends among the close-knit community where everyone seemed related to someone else and local schools were the centre of the town's life. Now that we were property magnates, however, Anne was determined to make her mark on our new abode, and that became evident when I surprised her with a long weekend trip to Paris and we were chatting over wine in a pavement café.

Intoxicated by the atmosphere as much as the sweet Cabernet, I made an extravagant gesture. 'Let me buy you something,' I said; 'something that will remind us of this trip.'

'Don't be silly,' said Anne. 'We can't afford to waste money. The house needs a lot doing to it.'

'No, honestly. Let me get you something: something to wear, perhaps, or jewellery. A painting? That way, we'll always have Paris.'

'Well, there is something I would like.'

'Name it and it's yours.' (The wine talking, obviously.)

'But we don't have to get it here. It can wait until we're home.'

'You're missing the point. This is about Paris and romance. What would you like?'

'A Black & Decker garden strimmer,' she said, adding helpfully, 'but they're on sale at the B&Q in Galashiels.'

Who says romance is dead?

5.

WIRELESS TOWERS

Let me surprise *you* now, dear reader, with a 7,000-mile trip across the Atlantic, to the west coast of America and to a small town in southern Oregon. With its picturesque setting and dark past, Coos Bay could easily be the location for a John Carpenter movie or those opening chapters of a Stephen King novel, where the viewer/reader is waiting to find out if, this time, it's the sheriff, the dog or the car that's been possessed by a demon. Clean, quiet and with inhabitants so spookily friendly that you just can't square it with the town's oddly tragic claims to fame: numerous shipwrecks and 'Oregon's only recorded lynching'. It's also home to K-Light, a little radio station housed in a two-storey, timber-framed house on the outskirts of town, next to a budget motel.

In the studio this morning, you would find Yours Truly as the guest on the breakfast show, chatting with the male and female hosts about, of all things, 1970s funny man Benny Hill.

'Jeff Zycinski joins us from the BBC in Scotland. Jeff, we all remember those great BBC TV shows like Benny Hill ...'

'Yes, that brings back memories.'

I didn't mention that it wasn't a BBC show, or that my memories of Benny Hill tended to be of double-speed chase scenes, where an old pervert drooled after young girls in bikinis. I didn't, because K-Light was one of the many Christian music stations that you could hear across the USA, and I wasn't even sure I could use phrases like 'scantily clad' at that time in the morning.

The visit to Coos Bay happened halfway through a fun road-trip that Anne and I took from Seattle to San Francisco. As she snoozed peacefully in the various hotels and motels, I popped in to different radio stations, gathering material for a Radio Scotland series called *Don't Touch that Dial*. James Boyle had given the go-ahead, even offering to pay the cost of the rented Chevrolet, but on the condition that it wouldn't spoil our holiday. Far from it, because those of us that work in radio can't travel anywhere without tuning in to the local stations. Having a reason to actually visit them was an anorak's dream.

'And *Upstairs, Downstairs,*' the male host said. 'That was another terrific show.'

'Indeed. A classic.'

And again, not a BBC show, but now was not the time to quibble.

'But,' said the female host, 'Why are *you* here, Jeff? Doesn't the BBC employ any women?'

Ah, the gentle warm-up was over and now we were off on a new tangent as I found myself describing the BBC's pre- and post-war employment policies and wondering why we hadn't got in to this sexism debate when we were reminiscing about Benny Hill. So far, there'd been no mention of God, which I also found odd, because that's really why I was there.

It was the mid-1990s and K-Light was aiming to attract an audience of younger listeners and woo teenagers away from the worst excesses of demonic rock, pop and house music.

'Who's in the house?' the jingles asked.

'Jesus is in the house!' the jingles answered.

Meanwhile, promos for its edgy talk show featured clips from a pro-life debate and the sound of a woman screaming, 'They're killing our babies!' It was powerful stuff and, despite my mauling on air, K-Light's programme director seemed genuinely pleased to have a visitor from Scotland and offered me a tour of the station. One thing that caught my eye was a rack of computer servers encased behind glass in the reception foyer. This, he told me, was another radio service, completely automated, which targeted older audiences with traditional church services and sermons. I wanted to know more about this: the technology, not the sermons. But I checked my watch and realised I was late for breakfast muffins with Anne and we'd need to get back on to the Pacific Coast Highway if we were going to keep to our schedule and make it to San Francisco the following day.

It had been a fascinating trip that started with KIRO, Seattle's well-regarded news and talk station, where I interviewed the news editor and the host of the morning phone-in show, who had just moved to KIRO from another station. This mobility of presenters (and indeed station bosses) was the first difference I noticed about the industry in America. When a show began to dip in the ratings, the presenters were told to pack their stuff in a box and they 'hauled ass' to another station, usually in a completely different part of the country and, therefore, a different radio market.

The biggest difference, though, was that presenters were allowed to be much more opinionated. Rush Limbaugh's tirades against Bill Clinton and the liberal elite were already being networked across the country, but even this Seattle morning host had no compunction about describing state lottery players as 'morons', or taking a few pot-shots at some budget overspend at City Hall. It made for a fiery listen, whereas in Britain the presenter set up a topic as provocatively as was permitted under broadcasting laws and waited for the callers to supply the opinions.

At this point I'm suddenly reminded of a St Andrew's Day phone-in on Radio Scotland, when Gary Robertson asked listeners to have a moan-free morning and tell him, very simply, what they loved about living in Scotland.

'Hello, Gary. I like Scotland because there are no scorpions here.'

'Scorpions?'

'Yes. You go to some of these hot countries in America or Africa and there are scorpions everywhere.'

'Ah, so one advantage of our colder climate, no creepy crawlies?'

'No, I'm just talking about scorpions.'

'I know, but I'm making the point that there are other creatures in those hotter countries.'

'All I'm saying is, I'm glad there are no scorpions. Just scorpions, I'm talking about. Scorpions.'

'So, you like living in Scotland because ...?'

'Because there are no scorpions. That's right.'

'Any other reason you like it here?'

'No. Just that. No scorpions.'

'Got it. Okay, next caller on the line is ...'

Coming back to scorpion-free Scotland after that American trip, it struck me how the comparatively few stations available on our dials – even in cities as large as Glasgow or Edinburgh – created some complacency. The so-called rivalry between the BBC and commercial radio amounted to little more than good-natured mocking. In Scotland there was little movement of audience between the BBC and commercial stations. If there was ever any threat to a BBC station it tended to come from another BBC station and, as I was discovering, there was so much back-stabbing going on between radio and television that it was no wonder the BBC had a full-time nurse at each of its main buildings. If people saw enemies, they were usually from within.

But all that seemed about to change with the launch of a brand-new service, based in Edinburgh, but broadcasting coast-to-coast across Central Scotland. It was promising a 50/50 split of music and high-quality speech and had the backing of two television companies, Grampian and Border TV. With that kind of broadcasting and business know-how behind it, surely it was going to be a serious contender for Radio Scotland's daytime listeners. It was to be called Scot FM.

I, meanwhile, was now back in Selkirk, typing out another batch of programme offers for the Head of Radio and, after making good on my Parisian promise of a new strimmer, admiring Anne's handiwork in our garden. Then came the call to go back north. Maggie Cunningham had recruited the author and columnist Tom Morton to host a new mid-morning show and came to Selkirk to ask if I would be interested in taking charge of the production team in Inverness. I threw my hat in the ring and went up to Glasgow for another interview, but this time I was much more relaxed. The job with Tom's show would not be a promoted post, but what made it interesting was the thought of running a chunk of the daytime schedule – albeit late morning – just as we were heading into battle with a new competitor. I mentioned this alongside my recent observations about the American market and was offered the job.

Anne was delighted, and we put our Selkirk house on the market expecting it might take weeks or months to sell. Luckily, just as the estate agent was hammering the 'For Sale' post into our beautifully strimmed front lawn, a local butcher knocked on the door and said he would give us our asking price without waiting for a surveyor's report, on condition that we moved out within four weeks. He was selling his business in town and, as he lived above the shop, needed a new place to live. We agreed and soon the removal van was whisking us and our furniture to Inverness.

Anne's delight was prompted partly by the thought of living in a bigger town with more to do and see, but also because she thought Inverness would be a good place to raise a family. Yes, our first child was on the way. Eight months later, at Raigmore Hospital, baby Sarah would make her entrance. In those intervening eight months I'd meet Tom Morton, get to know the production team, launch the show and through trial and many errors, learn about running a live daily programme, leading a team and understanding the complexities of a presenter's psyche.

Elsewhere on Radio Scotland, things had changed. Eddie Mair was now making a name for himself in London and in his vacated slot, various presenter combinations had been tried but found wanting. The production team that had bonded and worked so well behind Eddie began to break up as the editor, producers and researchers took up jobs elsewhere.

As Scot FM came on air, it was obvious that it would not live up to its promise of offering high-quality speech. Instead, its most notable offering was Scotty McClue's late-night phone-in show. This was the closest thing Scotland – or indeed Britain – had to a 'shock-jock'. Colin Lamont, an otherwise genial fellow with an interest in gardening, assumed the character of Scotty and riled his late-night listeners with thoughts on overpaid teachers and work-shy nurses. The station's early listening figures were disappointing and, in the Press, Scot FM inherited the prefix 'troubled', which had once been applied to the early days of Radio Scotland.

Tom Morton, meanwhile, had done enough in his early months to impress the Head of Radio and we got word that we would soon be given the more prestigious 0845–1000 slot that Eddie Mair had once made his own. Despite being sworn to secrecy about this plan, I stupidly shared it with the team and within minutes, news of our celebrations had reached the ears of our doomed colleagues in Glasgow. An angry James Boyle called me and demanded that I be in his office at nine sharp the next morning – presumably for a dressing-down.

A nine o'clock meeting in Glasgow meant setting the alarm clock for 5 a.m., being nudged onto the floor by Anne's ever-sharpening elbow, then a three-and-a-half-hour drive to Glasgow. No train could get me there earlier. At BBC Scotland HQ, I awaited the wrath of the boss, but James was all smiles and said he understood what had happened and ushered me out of his office, telling me that I could now go back to Inverness. I had been in that meeting for all of two minutes and, driving back up the A9, I realised that the seven-hour round trip had itself been my punishment.

It was now time to start planning for the all-new *Tom Morton Show*. It would be very different from the gentle mix of music and conversation that we had been producing thus far. It would be an all-speech magazine format with a mix of live interviews, celebrity guests and built features. I asked Judith MacKay, who had been part of Eddie Mair's team, to spend some weeks with us in the pre-launch period and she offered invaluable advice. There was a lot of interest in what we would do, and we had frequent visitors from the management team in Glasgow. On one occasion, the BBC's National Governor for Scotland, Norman Drummond, arrived in Inverness and very kindly invited Judith and me for lunch at the nearby Heathmount Hotel. Rather than quiz us about the new programme, he eloquently described his own career trajectory as a chaplain at Fettes College, then as headmaster at Loretto School. Before that, there had been his time in the Church of Scotland, doing what sounded very much like missionary work with street gangs in a Glasgow housing scheme. Which one? Easterhouse, of course.

'The trouble with those poor kids,' he told us, 'is that they had no hope, no aspirations, no ambition.'

I whispered to Judith to say nothing about my background, kicking her under the table when she couldn't resist the moment. 'Actually, Jeff was born in Easterhouse, weren't you, Jeff? What was it like having no hope or ambition?'

The National Governor looked a little ill at ease, so we moved on to talking about Tom Morton.

Tom himself played a big part in deciding the shape of his new programme, so too did Judith, and so did I. And there, with that obvious superfluousness of cooks, we made the broth. Tom, who had moved with his family to Shetland, commuted week in, week out to present the show and, rather than fork out on hotel rooms, he bought an old camper van, parked it in the rear car park at BBC Inverness and slept there three nights a week. An odd arrangement, but it certainly reduced the risk of him being late to the studio. On air he described Inverness as 'Dolphinsludge', which annoyed some locals, and dubbed our Culduthel Road studios 'Wireless Towers'.

Those early shows were hit and miss. With such a wide range of content there were often awkward gear changes from, say, a discussion on South African apartheid to the record-breaking attempts to eat baked beans with a cocktail stick. When a troupe of Russian performance artists appeared on air, Tom struggled on for five minutes before giving up: they couldn't understand his questions and he was equally baffled by their answers. This prompted a memorably pompous memo from the Head of Radio: 'It is surely incumbent upon the senior producer and researchers to ensure that guests who appear on Radio Scotland can actually speak in a language that can be understood by the majority of our listeners.' He had a point.

Looking back, I realise that we were trying to force Tom into the kind of format which Eddie Mair would have embraced with his sharp wit and slightly eccentric worldview. Tom was a different beast, and the more we got to know of his enthusiasms – different, but equally diverse – the more we created a show that worked for him.

Tom liked talking about books and films, motorbikes and rock music, religion and gadgets, and food. Like me, he had a natural curiosity for the minutiae of the world around him. Looking at a Post Office pillar box one day, we developed a short series of features telling the history of street furniture. A mention of typhoid in a news story inspired a weekly slot called *Deadly Diseases: Where are they now?* We spoofed those nostalgia monologues that ran on STV with our own *Teacake Tales* and *Tales from the Croft*. As our self-confidence grew, so did our sense of fun.

Threatened industrial action from the Musicians' Union prompted the production team to become a kazoo orchestra and replace the programme's normal signature tune with a harmonised kazoo arrangement of the theme from *The*

Muppet Show. Longer-lasting features included *Answers Back*: a conversation format in which celebrity guests discussed various aspects of their lives after being prompted by surprise messages left on an answering machine by friends and colleagues. These days we would call it 'voicemail'.

As a team leader I was on a steep learning curve and, to be honest, I had picked up some bad habits from my days in the Clyde newsroom. Initially I tried to manage the producers as I would a team of reporters: I told them to push their desks together into one big block, thinking this would make them operate as a unit and share ideas and suggestions for the programme, but all it really did was to raise the noise level so that phone conversations became virtually impossible.

My mistake here was in not immediately appreciating the strengths of each individual. Anne Bates, for example, had a passion for truly emotional human-interest stories. Mike Walker, who had created a small wall of travel guides around his desk, preferred stories about foreign climes and cars. Lamont Howie was a larger-than-life character with a sense of humour unfettered by notions of political correctness, and an easy familiarity with Scotland's landed gentry. Colin McPhail, who assured us he never watched television, was the intellectual backbone, researching in-depth topics such as pre-Millennium angst, global warming and the future of banking. Gillian Russell preferred lifestyle topics, and researcher Jan Byrne, a former schoolteacher, brought a hinterland of life experiences and a fascination for the legends of superstitions of the Highlands. Bruce McGregor, then a young musician, knew the traditional music scene, and Deirdre Leitch, newly graduated from Queen Margaret College, connected us with younger audiences and had a zeal for meticulous organising and planning.

I was fortunate to have such a team – part inherited, and part recruited – and like the *Eddie Mair Live* team in Glasgow, there grew a sense of solidarity and lasting friendship. As we expanded to meet the demands of an extended programme duration, freelance reporter Gareth Hydes came on board as a full-time producer and immediately began shooting for the moon. Hearing that former astronaut John Young was visiting Scotland, Gareth began weeks of protracted negotiations with NASA to have him as a guest on Tom's show. These discussions mainly involved the strict precautions that would have to be put in place to ensure the safety and security of this all-American hero. Gareth insisted all this would be worth the effort. John Young, after all, had been one of the few men to have stepped on the surface of the moon, he had flown the Space Shuttle and was still active within NASA, training a new generation of astronauts. Finally, the top guys in Florida gave their approval, but insisted that Young be collected from the airport by a BBC-vetted chauffeur.

John McCormick's driver – who is fast becoming a recurring character in these short memoirs – was pressed into service yet again: our astronaut was safely landed in the Radio Scotland studio and, as we went live, Tom asked him about those days on the moon.

'I'm not here to talk about that,' was the legend's response.

Tom, glancing through the studio glass to where Gareth sat in the control room, looked perplexed.

'I'm here in your country to promote the wider cause of science.'

Tom tried again. 'But surely your exploits on the Apollo missions are an inspiration?'

'Nope. Not talking about that.'

Gareth, his head in his hands, couldn't believe what he was hearing. I'm not saying this experience haunted him for the rest of his career, but if you mention anything about the moon to him, even now, he twitches slightly and points to hours and hours of YouTube content where John Young can be seen chatting happily about the moon and offering vivid descriptions of what he saw and what he felt.

We can only assume that damn driver said something to upset him.

Although the new Tom Morton programme was in its infancy, Anne and I had a real-life infant to look after once Sarah was born. In those early days of night feeds and inexplicable tears – I'm talking about me, not Sarah – I came to the office exhausted but determined to prove we could get things right. We knew there had been some talk in Glasgow about our various mishaps, but as I travelled with Maggie Cunningham to yet another programme review board, it dawned on us that our own, first, honest assessments had fuelled the belief that the programme wasn't working. Such was the culture of perpetual meetings in Glasgow that few people there actually had time to listen – they believed what we told them.

We decided, from then on, to praise Tom to the skies, talk up the strengths of the production team and tell everyone that the show was now 'rock solid'. We wondered how quickly this phrase would get back to us.

When the Head of Radio came to Inverness on his next routine visit, he praised the innovative features we had developed and even our ambitious quest for guests. He declared that Tom's ownership of the format was now 'rock solid'.

Then he asked us to take the show to Hollywood.

6.

REACHING FOR THE STARS

Hollywood, Los Angeles, is the movie capital of the world, the land of dreams and make-believe, but the events unfolding as I gunned the rental car along Sunset Boulevard were happening in reality. We were being followed and there was now no doubt of that.

I had spotted the tail in my mirrors shortly after we had eased out of the university parking lot. It was three in the morning; the middle of the night. The nearby freeway ramp was closed for overnight maintenance, but I had banked on the surface route from Hill Street to Hollywood being an easy one. There were few other cars on the road, just that black sedan that had been mimicking my every turn since we hit Chinatown. Using every technique I had learned from American cop shows, I tried to shake it off by turning, without blinkers, up side streets and jumping the lights at deserted cross-walks.

There was just no losing this guy.

As my speedometer needle inched upwards, he kept pace. I gave the gas pedal another squeeze, but he must have done the same. We had to get to the hotel and fast – it had an underground parking garage. Even if he followed us inside, we could dump the car and make a run for the stairwell that connected the garage to the reception hallway.

My mind was already racing with those vivid descriptions of knife attacks and drive-by shootings that we had heard about from the gang members. Had we done something to annoy them? Had they expected money in return for sharing their stories? Or had they simply seen us as an easy mark; those fools from Scotland who were crazy enough to be out on the streets when anyone with one iota of common sense would be locked down for the night?

All I knew was that I could not allow the black sedan to get closer and I mustn't let it come alongside. I cut off from Sunset and headed up towards Hollywood Boulevard. A few hours earlier, we had strolled along there with the tourists, checking out the golden stars on the Walk of Fame, enjoying the California sunshine. Jack Lemmon had died that day and his star had been marked with a wreath set on a wire-frame stand.

Now, it looked like a very different place.

Now everything looked dead.

Even the hookers had clocked off for the night and there were no LAPD patrols to flag down. We passed the Capitol Records building and then, approaching Hollywood and Highland, I caught sight of the Holiday Inn and the revolving restaurant on its roof. We were almost home, almost safe. But the black sedan was closer than ever.

It had been my idea to take the *Tom Morton Show* to Hollywood, but even as the suggestion popped out of my mouth, I knew I had no idea how to accomplish it. James Boyle had convened a meeting of Radio Scotland senior producers and we had gathered around the boardroom table in the BBC's Queen Street building. Each person in the room had responsibility for a particular programme or team and, because we were in Edinburgh, it was mainly the arts and culture set. James outlined his plan for a short season that would have a focus on film-making and then he went around the table to hear our ideas. The producer in charge of the book programme offered a special on film biographies and the senior producer of the Arts Programme suggested a special on film scores.

Had they known about the agenda in advance? Had I missed a memo? I realised I'd have to come up with something fast. Plan B involved jumping out of the window. It was not a great Plan B.

'What about you, Jeff. Any thoughts?'

I looked at the window.

'We were thinking …' I began, giving the impression that any thought had actually gone in to this, 'that we should take Tom to Hollywood for the week and do the programme from there.'

'Live or pre-recorded?' James asked.

I had no idea. 'Well, live, of course,' I said.

This provoked some smirks and sighs from the others. A science producer helpfully offered me a short lecture on the work of Nicolaus Copernicus and the rotation of the earth and pointed out the eight-hour time difference. To broadcast live at 9 a.m. in Scotland would mean starting at

1 a.m. in Los Angeles. We wouldn't be finished up until almost 3 a.m.

'Yes, we considered that,' I lied, 'but the advantage there is we can get use of a vacant studio in a radio station at that time. And it might be cheaper.'

James considered this while the smirking among the others reached competitive levels.

'Sounds good,' he said. The smirks vanished.

The initial excitement among the Inverness team subsided when I said plainly that we couldn't afford to take everyone across the Atlantic. Besides, we would need people back at base to bring in the link from LA and relay it to Glasgow. I selected producers and researchers who I thought would be able to do a quick fix on guests and stories if others let us down, and I asked John Carmichael, one of the sound engineers in Inverness, to join us. But I still felt short of on-the-ground knowledge and the obvious person to ask was Carol Wightman, the producer of Radio Scotland's travel programme, *A Case for Packing*. She had produced a recent network documentary on American gang culture and had contacts in the tougher neighbourhoods of Los Angeles.

Maybe it was something to do with my own upbringing, but that kind of story interested me a lot more than just the obvious stuff about stars and showbiz. Naturally we would cover the glitz and glamour too. This was for Radio Scotland's Movie Week, after all.

Six of us flew to Hollywood for the nine-day trip, the last four of which would include the live broadcasts from the studios of KUSC, a university radio station that played highbrow classical and jazz music in daytime hours.

We checked in to the Holiday Inn. It was within walking distance from the main strip and the famous Chinese Theatre with its palm-prints of stars embedded in the concrete forecourt. Each morning, after breakfast in the hotel's dining room, I would ask the entire team to pull up chairs and gather round as we mapped out the day's assignments and decided who was going where. Although the shows would be live, we needed a fair number of pre-recorded inserts to give the listeners that sense of place, and also because it was unlikely we could persuade many big names to join us live in the studio in the early hours.

Once things were sorted, the others went back to their rooms to fetch bags and jackets, while I sat finishing my coffee and ticking off a checklist of things that needed to be done. Each morning, it was the same waitress who would clear our plates and, because I was afraid of getting it wrong, I'd tip her far too generously, slapping five-dollar bills around like it was Monopoly money. I could see that she was curious about us and had watched as we rifled through reams of briefing notes and production schedules, checking microphones and recording equipment were in working order. The third morning in, she finally asked me what we were doing.

'We're from the BBC in Scotland,' I told her, 'We're preparing some radio shows for next week'

'So, you're from the BBC, huh?'

'Yes. BBC Radio.'

She thought about this for a moment and then revealed the real reason for her approach.

'I don't know if you're interested or not, but I've been in a few movies myself.'

I looked at her more closely, wondering if I should recognise her.

'Anything I might have seen?' I asked.

'Maybe. They're what you might call, artsy movies.'

'I see.'

'If you like, I could arrange a screening for you.'

'A screening? You mean at a cinema? I mean, a movie theatre?'

I was already picking up the lingo.

'No, silly, I mean here at the hotel. I could hook up a VCR in one of the rooms.'

'Well, I don't know. You say this is an arthouse film?'

'Yeah, kinda, if you don't mind a bit of nudity. You know, just folks doing what nature intended. And there are horses.'

'Oh. It's a western?'

She laughed.

'Yeah, well, you could say that. It gets pretty wild.'

Just then the others came back and I apologised, saying that I had to go because I was one of the drivers on duty that day.

'Catch you later then,' she called after me cheerily.

I never did get that private screening, but the incident was one of many that reminded me that this really was an industry town and everyone seemed connected with the business in one way or another.

As half of our group went out to record interviews, I went with John to see the studio we would be using for the live broadcasts. Waiting for us there was Hank, the local sound guy, who turned out to be one of the university's technicians. He had installed the control desk himself and flushed with pride when John told him how good it was. It was like getting the seal of approval from the BBC itself. But as soon as Hank was out of the door, John's smile faded and he opened his bag of tools and cables and slid under the desk.

'I may be some time,' were his last words before he disappeared completely.

Over the next four hours, John stripped out wiring and rerouted circuits. From time to time, Hank would pop his head around the door, looking increasingly concerned at the spaghetti mess of cable that John was leaving in his wake, but he said nothing. When it was over, John declared the studio was now fit for our purpose and we would have no problem linking up with Inverness and broadcasting Tom's show to the nation. Whether that studio would be fit for its original purpose after we left, I didn't dare ask.

As we were doing this, the other half of the team was with Tom, recording interviews with the likes of actor Michael York and, in a long, dark bar off Sunset, tracking down a man from Glasgow's Shettleston area who now scratched a living by writing treatments for potential movies. These treatments never saw the light of day as actual films but had been optioned enough times that he could keep himself in pizza and beer.

We then started to close in on some of the bigger names. The actor Ed Asner agreed to be interviewed in his office and, although I usually let Tom do all the talking in these situations, the actor latched on to my Polish surname during our introductions and asked about my family history as he told us about his own parents, who were of Russian origin. All the while, during that conversation, I kept thinking to myself that this was the guy who played Lou Grant – *Lou Grant*! – the programme that had first got me interested in being a journalist.

Legendary screen star Gregory Peck, meanwhile, thought it would be a good idea to record the interview with him on the lawn of his large estate in West Los Angeles. Pausing to allow the noise of an overhead helicopter to subside, he then told us about the time he had seen a dozen or more choppers blacken the sky as they ferried fully grown fir trees to a nearby neighbour. It was December, Peck explained, and his neighbour wanted to create a forest of Christmas trees in his garden. When you have that kind of money, you really don't have to wait for nature to take its course. Despite warnings that he might be cold and aloof, Gregory Peck was a generous host and a great interviewee. He talked about his favourite role as Atticus Finch from *To Kill a Mocking Bird* and, long before smartphones and selfies became a thing, he allowed producer Anne Bates to create her own special memory of the occasion by holding the Oscar he had won for that role.

Another memorable interview came backstage in the green room of the *Tonight Show* where, after host Jay Leno had said his thanks to guest Charlton Heston, he met us to talk about his grandmother. She, it turned out, was from Greenock and Leno couldn't resist doing a Scottish accent as authentic as that of Scotty in the original *Star Trek* series. He had his own thoughts about fame and show business: as a child he'd watched Johnny Carson present the *Tonight Show* and was always disappointed when Johnny took time off and a substitute presenter was put in place. Leno said he took as little time off as possible and that he enjoyed meeting fans of the show at any time, in any place, because, as he put it, 'Every handshake is another viewer.'

I was thinking about that the next afternoon when Tom and I were having lunch in Hamburger Hamlet on Hollywood Boulevard. A young man approached our table and, talking directly to me, but flicking a thumb back to the table he had just left, said, 'Excuse me, sir. I'm wondering if you could settle a bet between me and my girlfriend.'

I looked over at her. She smiled and waved. I waved back.

'I'll try,' I said.

'I told her you were someone famous, but she doesn't agree.'

'Who do you think I am?'

I was hoping for the likes of Tom Cruise, Harrison Ford, or maybe one of the older gang like Redford or Newman.

'Well, I say you're that guy who makes those documentaries. Michael Moore, is it?'

'It is,' I said, 'but I'm not him.'

He was crestfallen, but then immediately doubtful and I could see he was thinking that Michael Moore probably got this kind of annoying interruption every time he sat down to eat and, if you were him and wanted a quiet life, wouldn't you deny being Michael Moore? He was, after all, famous for his sense of humour.

'You *sure* you're not him?' said the young man, his eyes narrowing.

'Quite sure. Sorry.'

'But, it's just that ...' and here he pointed to my arms, 'You're wearing two wristwatches, so I thought ...'

'No. Sorry. I just like to know the time here and in Scotland,' I explained without context. If I mentioned anything about making programmes he was just going to get more suspicious. He apologised for taking up our time and wandered back to his girlfriend with the news. She immediately shrieked and I saw him unfolding dollar bills from his wallet.

Before we left Hamburger Hamlet, I went to the restroom and looked at myself in the mirror. I was wearing glasses, a baseball cap and a Hollywood t-shirt with the logo of a silent-era camera surrounded by stars. I looked a *little* like Michael Moore, but I looked much more like the character they always arrested by mistake in movies about serial killers: not the killer himself, but the creepy, fat guy that lived in his mom's basement eating Twinkies – the wrong guy. Not Michael Moore and not even the main psycho. That guy!

By the end of the week, and after three programmes successfully beamed back to Scotland, we felt we had offered listeners a good slice of Hollywood life, from the rich and famous to the down at heel. Tom's observations about the shopping-cart poor were recognisable to us all. Carol Wightman, who, it seemed, had gone undercover into the back streets of Compton, now emerged and told us she had secured real-life gang members who had agreed to be at the KUSC studio at 1 a.m. for the final show.

I don't think everyone was as thrilled about this as Carol was; certainly not the station's security patrol who called to say that our special guests had arrived with an entourage of friends in tow.

Tom's interview was hard-hitting but truly touching, as we heard vivid descriptions of gang life in Compton and how so many friends and family members had been lost to the gun or the knife. For this final show, I was producing from the control room, listening intently to these tales of tragedy, ever mindful we were going out live to a morning audience in Scotland, and hoping these hard-bitten gang members would heed my pleas about bad language. They did. The clock counted down the minutes and seconds and then we brought up the signature tune and handed over to the news bulletin in Glasgow. That was a wrap. We closed the faders and breathed a sigh of relief.

It was time to pack our stuff, say our 'thank yous' to the kind people who had allowed us to use their studio and *improve* their circuitry, and then head back to the hotel for a celebratory drink before collapsing into bed. What I didn't know was what had been happening in the production office outside the studio. There the leather and denim-clad 'entourage' had been becoming restless and some had even convinced the others that this whole thing was a set-up, a con job, an FBI sting operation designed to ensnare one or more of them with outstanding arrest warrants. Although our team had tried to keep them calm and divert them with questions about their various tattoos, the university's security guard was giving them the once-over and wondering aloud whether he should frisk them. John Carmichael pointed out that it might be a little late for that.

As we came off air, it was all smiles and high-fives as those who had been interviewed seemed to have enjoyed the experience, and thanked Tom for, 'You know, giving a goddamn.'

We said our farewells, but it was on that journey back across the dead streets of Los Angeles that I noticed the car behind me flashing its headlights and tracking my route across town as I zig-zagged my way to the hotel's parking garage. Despite my best efforts, the black sedan pulled up alongside. The driver's window slid down and an angry man asked me why I had been driving like a madman.

It was John Carmichael driving our other rental car and trying to keep pace with us to make sure we got back safely. He too had been spooked by all that talk of street killing and drive-by shootings.

I should have realised, but it had been a long week.

A day later, we were back in Inverness and Tom's next encounter with a big star would not be so happy.

7.

A STAR IN THE NORTH

After three years of marriage, Anne had perfected her technique of early morning elbow-nudging, but that morning I needed a second nudge to get me moving.

'Go and see what he's like in real life,' she urged. 'I want a full report when you get home. Ask him if he likes Inverness. Where do you think he'll be staying? Will you be going to the pub with him? He likes a drink. Don't bring him back here; the house is a mess. Sarah's toys are everywhere.'

To be fair, Anne's excitement about Chris Evans was shared by many people that week. As the host of Radio 1's *Breakfast Show*, his antics on and off air often made headlines in the tabloid press. Recently, after telling his listeners that he needed to escape the smoke and grime of London, and then dropping hints about where he might go, he had finally revealed the location for his two-week getaway. The Highlands of Scotland, he said, would give him and his studio posse a huge gulp of much-needed fresh air and, the following week, he would present his show from the BBC's 'clockwork studio' in Inverness.

That weekend a courier firm started to deliver production boxes of tapes and equipment and it dawned on us that this would be a great publicity opportunity for BBC Scotland, as well as Radio 1. Our Culduthel Road studios were located in a Victorian town house that had been converted and expanded in the 1970s to house teams from Radio Scotland and Radio nan Gàidheal. Despite the passing of the decades, I suspected many local people – especially teenagers – had no idea we were there: ten days of Radio 1 glitz would put us on the map.

I made my way into the office determined, if nothing else, to gather enough behind-the-scenes details to satisfy Anne's curiosity. That evening I had little to report.

'So, what was he like?'

'Never saw him,' I admitted. 'He came in just before six. He played a Kenneth McKellar record, did his show and then had a meeting with his team. I think he signed a few autographs for girls hanging about outside.'

'Oh, is that all?'

'Well, the cleaners are miffed.'

'Why?'

'They wished him good morning and they say he ignored them.'

Anne tried to find an excuse for this rudeness. Her apparent fondness for Radio 1's breakfast boy made me suspect she was not the devoted listener to Radio Scotland's *Good Morning Scotland* that she had hitherto made out.

'Were they speaking Gaelic?' she asked, hopefully.

'I don't think so.'

As the days passed, my reports didn't improve much and, as Tom Morton returned from his own two-week break, I was in hot water with him because of an article I'd written for *The Scotsman*. The paper had asked me to dash out a few hundred words describing the preparations for Chris Evans' first show. Struggling to say much more than 'Some boxes have arrived,' I had called shops and businesses around town to gather some quotes. A city barber offered to cut the DJ's famous tousled ginger locks and a local nightclub manager said that, 'Yes, it would be *quite nice* if he popped in.' Thrilling stuff.

Desperate to make the word count, I had added some pathetic joke about Chris and Tom having similar silly specs. Tom was not amused. I blamed *The Scotsman*. It was subbed badly, I told him, but he wasn't convinced. Still, there was the promise of Chris Evans appearing on Tom's show later in the week and, for all that he may have been a bit surly inside the building, on air he was effusive about the delights on offer in this part of Scotland. He even talked about moving to the Highlands permanently and suggested his London listeners do likewise as he read out a list of house prices in and around Inverness.

At that time, it was said you could sell a damp-ridden flat in London and buy a castle in the Highlands. It was this kind of comment which slowly but surely started to irritate listeners in Scotland and ran the risk of resurrecting old arguments about the so-called 'white settlers' who could wreck local communities by purchasing holiday homes in small villages. By the end of his third day, Anne had stopped asking for reports, but I updated her anyway.

'A Gaelic presenter says one of Chris Evans' team tried to run him down in the car park. Or was it the other way around? Depends who you believe. Oh, and lots of stuff keeps being delivered for them: Barr's Irn-Bru, Tunnock's teacakes – that kind of thing.'

'I thought BBC shows couldn't accept things like that. Will he have to send them back?'

I shrugged. I doubted it. Tom Morton had once made an unscripted reference to the Le Creuset brand on air and had received a casserole dish from the firm as a thank you. I had been a bit of a jobsworth about the whole thing and told him he could only keep it if he paid for it. I couldn't imagine Chris Evans or the Controller of Radio 1 getting worked up about fizzy drinks and chocolate biscuits.

By the Friday, Anne told me to stop talking about Chris Evans altogether. The novelty had worn off.

Had he gone back to London that weekend, the Chris Evans sojourn to the north would have been hailed as a triumph. Okay, he hadn't come around the building to shake our hands and thank us for accommodating him, but there was no law that said he had to. It was what he did on air that was important and, for the most part, that had gone really well.

Then came his second week.

My old pals and colleagues over at Moray Firth Radio had been watching and listening to the week's events and I suppose someone there thought it might be a good idea if they could grab a little piece of the action. Tich McCooey, the breakfast show presenter and a local legend, staged a surprise 'Fancy meeting you here' encounter with Evans at a hotel in Nairn. Just like the BBC cleaners, he was swept aside.

The next morning, however, a whole section of the Radio 1 Breakfast Show was devoted to the incident. Evans set about belittling Tich McCooey and pointing out – in case he hadn't checked his pay packet lately – that even Radio 1's youngest researchers were earning more than him. This was not a game, said Evans, it was a war.

All of this was said with not the slightest hint of humour. For listeners, this was not a fun way to wake up and start your day. There was an angry man on a big BBC radio station having a go at some poor sod on a local station that was so small that the managing director often said his patch had more sheep than listeners. Over at Moray Firth's Scorguie studios, I'm told a hush fell over every office as they listened to this tirade. I know that was the case in our Radio Scotland office, and I'm willing to bet it was a similar scene at Broadcasting House in London.

In that one outburst, Chris had created a David and Goliath situation, and no one ever supports poor old Goliath. The press articles which, until then, had been fairly positive, now took a sour turn. Jokes that Chris and his team had made about local girls as 'tartan tottie' were now quoted as proof of his arrogance and misogyny. Tich McCooey, meanwhile, played a blinder by turning the tables on Radio 1 and presenting his show from London, hobnobbing with pop stars and celebrities at Stringfellows night club. The London papers lapped it up.

The BBC was desperate to turn things around and I got a call from Glasgow asking if I could do anything to keep the press sweet. My efforts only caused more trouble. After drinks with one London newspaperman, I invited him and his photographer to grab some pictures of Tom Morton broadcasting from one studio, as the Radio 1 *Breakfast Show* beamed out from the one next door. The camera flashes set off panic among the Evans team. They covered the connecting window with books and newspapers, shielding themselves from further intrusion, and it was no surprise when they cancelled plans for Chris to appear on Tom's show. The official reason was that Chris had 'an important meeting with his financial advisers'.

That night, despite my promise to say no more, I described the day's events to Anne. The BBC had seized disaster from the jaws of triumph and I had played my own small role in the week's catastrophe. I slumped in an armchair. Anne was sympathetic.

'You've had better days then?' she said. 'I'll fetch the whisky.'

Tom himself put the tin lid on that second week by penning his own article for *The Scotsman* in which he went to town on this interloper from the south. Some of what he wrote hit the mark, although I thought comparing Chris Evans to 'the man who had master-minded the Highland Clearances' was just a bit over the top.

On the last Friday, Chris Evans said goodbye to Scotland and went back to London. He soon fell out of love with the BBC and took a job with Richard Branson's Virgin Radio. He liked it there so much he bought the station. Then he sold it to Scottish Media Group and a year after that they dispensed with his services. He returned to the BBC and had the tricky job of taking over from Terry Wogan on Radio 2, but he had eight years of success before announcing he was going back to Virgin.

In press interviews he now claims he's a very different person from the bad boy he was back in those old Radio 1 days.

Anne says she never listens to him.

I almost believe her.

8.

THE PRICE OF FISH

I'm sure Sigmund Freud would have something to say about my capacity for self-sabotage at crucial moments. Mind you, my German is patchy, so unless he was offering beer, schnitzel and a return train ticket to Munich, I wouldn't have a clue what he meant. But let's give my subconscious the benefit of the doubt as I recount the day Maggie Cunningham took me for an important lunch to discuss my ambitions for the future.

Maggie was about to move on from her job as Campus Editor in Inverness and take up a prestigious post as Secretary to the National Governor, Norman Drummond. She was already tiring of the lame jokes about her shorthand and typing skills. A few days before she packed her bags, she booked a table for two at the Heathmount so that she could help me map the next stage of my career. It was one of those crisp, sunny days in Inverness: shirt-sleeve weather and no jacket or tie required as I joined her for the ten-minute stroll to the hotel. A career chat indeed! It all felt very grown-up.

Those who know me will confirm that, when nervous or excited, I tend to speak with my hands almost as much as I bump my gums: I make wild, sweeping gestures to signify the potential of good ideas; I deploy both palms to suggest things that must stop; I chuck a thumb behind my shoulder to illustrate other locations. For good measure, I can throw in a few forehead slaps to reinforce embarrassment, disappointment or forgetfulness, depending on the strength of the slap. Given this tendency for animation, ordering a main course of liver, onions and rich gravy was not a good choice. Sure enough, within the first few minutes of serious conversation, my windmill hands had struck the fork on my plate. A baby potato acted as a sneaky fulcrum and the downward force leveraged a good-sized smattering of the brown juice and onion strips towards the front of my blue shirt. I made an immediate dash to the Gents to clean up and this is where 'Inner Jeff' took control.

Dabbing the gravy blobs with tap water wasn't having much impact so I filled the basin, removed the entire shirt and gave it the kind of rapid rinse and soap scrub that would have made a Ganges *dhobi* proud. The stain faded but the cotton was now saturated. Phase two of my cunning plan was to blast it quickly under the hand dryer. As I stood there, topless, holding my sodden shirt, I realised something was missing: there was no hand dryer, just paper towels. Catching sight of myself in the mirror, I mouthed a silent 'You idiot!' to my absurd reflection.

The guy in the mirror simply slapped his forehead and then slipped his arms into the soaking, wrinkled sleeves. Back at the table, I shivered and dripped through the rest of the conversation. Maggie appeared not to have noticed anything amiss, but there wasn't much talk about my career after that. And we skipped dessert.

I remained in charge of Tom Morton's show for another two years until a health scare easily convinced him to spend less time in a BBC car park and more time with his family in Shetland. His departure prompted another reworking of the daytime schedule. By this time, James Boyle had gone south to become Controller of Radio 4, and the Head of Radio post was scrapped.

Like elsewhere across the BBC, programme commissioning was being separated from production and I would now report, via the Head of North in Aberdeen, to the Head of Production in Glasgow, and thereafter to the Managing Editor for Radio, and thence to the new Head of Broadcast, Ken MacQuarrie. He scheduled comedian Fred MacAulay's showbiz and chat format after *Good Morning Scotland*. This was to be produced in Glasgow and the Inverness team was asked to develop a daily strand for our old eleven o'clock slot.

My new boss in Aberdeen chose Mark Stephen as the presenter, and the brief was to steer clear of topics that would be covered by other programmes, such as news, sport, music, lifestyle, entertainment and science. That didn't leave much to pick over and, already feeling we were going backwards, I was determined not to be pushed into the box marked 'couthy nostalgia'.

Inevitably we found ourselves earmarking any kind of story that had a connection with Scotland and, after offering a shortlist of alternatives to HQ, the programme was billed as *The Scottish Connection*. Attempts to maintain a contemporary edge led us to create regular features like *Scotland on the Web*, and John Carmichael showed us a new box of tricks – The Vectra Hotline – that could convert ordinary phone lines into good-quality outside broadcast lines so that we could get live reports from locations almost anywhere in Scotland. We dubbed it the 'hot box' and I put it through its paces by taking it up to the Cairngorm Ski Centre and broadcasting live from the top of a mountain.

I can't say I ever enjoyed overseeing this format, with an agenda always teetering on the edge of parochialism, but there was much at home to divert my attention. Anne was pregnant again and, two years after Sarah's appearance, baby Alan came into the world with his wide eyes and voracious appetite. Anne insisted the eyes were a sign of intelligence, inherited from her. She didn't directly apportion blame for his appetite, but I knew what she was getting at.

To keep my brain ticking over, I took time away from *The Scottish Connection* to make stand-alone features. One such included *The Eastern Promise*, where I returned to my childhood haunts in Easterhouse and told the story of how this gleaming new council scheme had been built to house families from Glasgow's decaying tenements but had then developed a reputation for gang violence and vandalism. Between interviews with long-time residents and local police, I had parked in front of my old primary school (now closed and shuttered) and was listening to Radio Scotland when news came through of a shooting at a primary school in Dunblane. To my surprise, the station did not stick with the story, but returned to the scheduled programme about Jimmy McGregor's trip along the Crinan Canal.

I switched to BBC Radio 5 Live and there, hour by hour, the horror unfolded: sixteen children and their teacher shot dead. I never got to the bottom of why Radio Scotland had not gone immediately to rolling news, but it was said that all the senior news people had gone into a meeting to discuss the television coverage and there was no one around with enough authority to dump the radio schedule. This was something I would remember in later years.

My opportunity to take up a new challenge came with the dawn of multimedia production at BBC Scotland. Vacancies were advertised for two new editors reporting to the Head of Features, Liz Scott. She was a no-nonsense woman who had built BBC Scotland's reputation for children's television programmes, such as *Fully Booked* and *The Singing Kettle.* In the restructuring, she had inherited a whole tranche of Radio Scotland's speech programmes, together with the radio output being produced for the UK networks.

I applied successfully for the job as Editor, Topical, in Glasgow, and Jane Fowler became the Editor for Features, in Edinburgh. It meant a move back to Glasgow for the growing Zycinski clan and there were tears as we drove out past streets where we had pushed Alan's pram or taken Sarah's hand to visit the local park. On the bright side, we would be closer to Anne's parents and to my dad, who was now in his eighties and, after two near misses, had reached the stage of relinquishing his car keys.

In this new multimedia approach to programme-making, my new job would come to encompass television as well as radio, and so a small group of us radio diehards was sent to the BBC's Elstree studios for a week-long crash course in television production. At that time, it was the home of *Top of the Pops* and it was fun walking through the gates each morning as screaming music fans waited for glimpses of their idols.

Some of what we were taught on the course was familiar to me from my student days in Cardiff – operating a studio TV camera and reading from an autocue – but I was captivated by the Avid system for editing video footage on computer screens. I couldn't wait to get my hands on the kit and, after a few hours, it struck me that in many ways it was easier than editing sound, because the pictures themselves provided natural cues. Years of watching television as a simple viewer had already equipped us with a sense of what looked right and what didn't. I soon realised that any image on screen would become tiresome to the eye if it remained there for more than five or six seconds.

The Elstree trip was also memorable because our week there coincided with two major events: the referendum on Scottish devolution was already underway before we set off, but by the time we hit London, campaigning had been suspended because of tragic events in Paris – Princess Diana had been killed in a car crash alongside Dodi Al Fayed.

To say that the city was in mourning would be to understate things. Every shop, it seemed, displayed pictures of the Princess, often adorned with a black ribbon. One afternoon, after coursework, a few of us caught the train into town and I took a walk into Kensington Palace Gardens where hundreds of mourners had been laying bouquets and wreaths. The scenes were unreal: people young and old, children, business types and tourists all gathering to pay tribute with expressions of grief you would associate with the loss of a close family member.

Being away from Scotland that week, I had no real sense, other than phone calls to Anne, about the reaction back home. She told me there had been some debate in the media about whether or not a Scotland football game should go ahead on the day of Diana's funeral. In the end, it didn't, but in London, in this bizarre mix of sorrow and pride, such a thing would never have been considered. There was no doubt that this was a different country and, if proof were needed, it came at the end of that week with the vote on devolution. Scotland voted 'yes'. There would be a Scottish Parliament.

Back in Glasgow, our newfound TV skills were soon put to the test when the BBC launched two new digital television channels: BBC Knowledge and BBC Choice. The latter would have an evening opt-out version in Wales, Northern Ireland and Scotland, which would include a news programme, *Newsline*, and, four nights a week, a wide-ranging discussion show called *Late Flyte*.

The funds available for BBC Choice Scotland were smaller even than those for radio, and it wasn't hard to see why existing television producers had not been keen to get involved. Nor, at that time, was there much evidence to suggest that viewers actually wanted such a service and, if they did, there were some difficulties in seeing it. Even existing satellite TV viewers had to convert to BSkyB's digital boxes and dishes to get these new services. Naturally, I was one of the early adopters and was immediately disappointed to discover that, while I could see a smattering of new UK channels, I was now blocked from viewing all those strange German and Italian soap operas that had held my gaze while bottle-feeding Sarah and Alan in the middle of the night.

Ewan Angus, as Head of Television Commissioning, was in ultimate control of the project and quickly arrived at the decision to invest more cash in fewer programmes so that the level of quality could be raised. The nightly *Late Flyte* became a once-a-week edition of *The Flyer*, and presenters such as Davie Scott, Lindsay Hill and Hannah McGill were now able to punctuate guest interviews with some illustrative clips of films and, joy of joy, specially shot location reports.

As an experiment, it was a useful testing ground for on- and off-screen talent and provided proof that viewers were interested in specific programmes rather than channels themselves. It also gave me my one claim to fame because, during those years as Editor of *Late Flyte*, I was responsible for more hours of non-news television than anyone else at BBC Scotland. Just a pity hardly anyone was watching.

Back in my comfort zone, Ken MacQuarrie had asked Liz Scott to develop a lunchtime phone-in show for Radio Scotland to be hosted by Lesley Riddoch. As devolution plans began to take shape, it was expected the people of Scotland would have a lot to say about it and a lot of questions for the politicians. Liz asked me to meet with Lesley and come up with some ideas. As an experienced journalist and broadcaster, Lesley was interested in doing more than, as she put it, 'Rattling a few cages and getting the phones ringing'. Likewise, I was keen that, in the new political landscape that was unfolding, we heard from people across the country and not just the chattering classes of Glasgow and Edinburgh.

Once again, I made the call to Judith MacKay. She had worked with Lesley some years past but was now with BBC News in London. The devolution vote had also made her interested in returning to Scotland. She, in turn, persuaded Gary Robertson to return from Radio 5 Live to become Lesley's news partner, reading the bulletins at the top of the hour and on the half-hour. As Judith took charge of editorial content, I went to see Ken MacQuarrie with my ambitious plan to ensure the programme got out of Glasgow as often as possible.

A call with John Carmichael had given me the information I needed on satellite links and I suggested to Ken that we create a mobile studio for Lesley so that she could travel the country and elicit voices and opinions from far and wide. He was enthusiastic, and we handed the mission to our Resources staff, who came up with a cost-effective solution for converting a camper van into a radio studio, while a separate transit van would be equipped with a state-of-the-art mixing desk and satellite dish.

There was one hiccup even before we got to the launch date. Judith had been keen to clear the schedule of some historic clutter, which had included a daily list of the fish prices at the various landing ports around the Scottish coast. This lunchtime recitation of herring, lemon sole and cod prices had become, to some observers, as poetic as the Shipping Forecast on Radio 4.

News of our intention to scrap it leaked out and various politicians in fishing constituencies, including the Banff and Buchan MP, Alex Salmond, denounced the plan. We put it on hold while our news colleagues in Aberdeen helpfully consulted with fishing-boat captains. Such vessels were now equipped with sophisticated communication gear and not a single one of them still relied on Radio Scotland to tell them where to land their catch. On that topic, at least, the politicians fell silent.

Lesley Riddoch's new programme was launched onto the airwaves sounding confident from the start, and within months the listening figures would confirm its success. A new Scottish Parliament was on its way and the people of Scotland soon had plenty to say about the decision-makers in Edinburgh. Donald Dewar became Scotland's First Minister in a Coalition Government and, as we approached the end of one millennium and looked ahead to the next, opposition leader Alex Salmond had bigger fish to fry.

Mention of the Millennium reminds me of the entire industry that sprang up to protect us from the perils of Y2K, and the large blue stickers on every office computer that had been checked and made safe from the 'Millennium Bug'. I remember the particular doomsday merchant who came in to check my laptop. He didn't appreciate me making light of the whole thing and, after a long, hard stare, painted a picture of planes falling from the sky, motorway pile-ups and hospital operations conducted by candlelight.

'And don't expect to see any of this on the news,' he continued, 'because there will be no TV stations on the air.'

'Ah, there's always a silver lining,' I said, provoking a stare that was longer and harder than the last one.

The fear of a broadcasting blackout did necessitate contingency plans. While I worked with producer Margaret-Anne Docherty on a fun-filled Hogmanay programme to celebrate the new era as it dawned, hour by hour, across the globe, others were being instructed on how to establish an emergency radio service should the bug bite.

Tony Currie, late of Radio Clyde and now a BBC continuity announcer, was posted to the massive Blackhill Transmitter between Glasgow and Edinburgh. There, if the worst happened, he would lock himself in a little cabin beneath the huge pylon and transmit any information that could be relayed to him from the emergency services. Knowing Tony, he would probably have interspersed this with a few cheery tunes and a mystery voice competition. As Scotland's winter weather kicked in, Tony was warned that lethal icicles could form on the transmitter's overhead struts and come crashing to the ground at any time. This was a hard-hat area, he told me, but of course the hard hats were stored inside the cabin. It was going to be a risky sprint.

As we all know, the Millennium Bug turned out to be a damp squib. Perhaps the doomsayers had done a good job of protecting us all and their efforts were worth the many millions of pounds they received for doing so. There was, however, some suspicion when these same people hinted that they had got the date wrong and it was really the end of March we needed to worry about.

As we say in Scotland, 'Aye, right!'

9.

THE BIG BOSS

I have often wondered what it must be like to be in charge of the entire BBC. Does it look as wonderfully eccentric and chaotic from the top of the tree as it seems to be for those of us swinging on the lower branches? Maybe, up there, it all makes perfect sense and it's like that sinister song 'From a Distance'. What exactly is that song saying about God? Does the world look beautiful because God is too far away to notice all the wars, poverty and starvation? If so, that seems to be letting Him off the hook somewhat.

The god-like figure charged with running the BBC is called the Director General and I've been on first-name terms with a few of them. That's not saying much, of course, because all the recent DGs liked to emulate a Steve Jobs persona of informality and insisted that you call them Tony, Greg or Mark. This was designed to foster the idea that they were just one of the team and that we should ignore the fancy office and six-figure salary.

The first DG of my BBC years was John – now Lord – Birt, who I saw in the flesh when I attended an *Extending Choice* session in London. This was one of those gentle brainwashing gatherings where the concept of offering distinctive content was explained yet again to a fairly large group of department editors and middle managers drawn from the different divisions across the UK. After the inevitable PowerPoint presentation, those of us who still had the will to live took part in a discussion, ignited by the following question: Which department of the BBC is the most important?

Naturally the folk from BBC News immediately laid claim to that one and, as far as they were concerned, there was not really any need for further debate. *Surely*, they thought, *we can now move on to the coffee and sandwiches*? Trouble was, the BBC Resources team then pointed out that, without their supply of technical know-how, no one would actually see or hear the programmes that were being made. Fair point. Hold the coffee. Then came a forceful – almost hysterical – argument from the department charged with collecting the licence fee and ensuring the BBC had enough revenue to keep the doors open and the transmitters buzzing. I think their argument was supercharged with frustration because people inside the Beeb tended to think of these guys as an invisible force of necessary evil, and people outside probably imagined that these were the nerdy blokes who sat inside old-fashioned TV detector vans, patrolling the streets of an evening for licence-fee evaders.

I'm not sure if the debate ever came to any conclusions and I don't think there was a vote on the issue. I'm assuming the point we were supposed to get was that every department of the BBC was vital to its success, but if there *had* been a vote most people would have voted for themselves and that says something about the levels of team spirit and collegiate cooperation that existed at that time.

John Birt then turned up with his spiel about the need for a digital vision for the BBC. As ever, he was logical and convincing and what he actually put in place would benefit every one of his successors. However, Birt had the impatient air of a man who would rather be somewhere else. He stayed long enough to take questions from the assembled staff, although his answers tended to question the need for the question and, in some cases, the questioner. One hapless chap from News adopted an unfortunate hectoring style as he quizzed the DG about the BBC's 24-hour News channel. Why had this launched before it was ready? Why the rush? Surely the early mistakes on air were proof that it had needed more time? Surely we'd just given ammunition to the critics?

After insisting the launch had not been rushed, John Birt quickly tired of this barrage of impudence and, much like the German navy captain in that famous episode of *Dad's Army*, he pulled out a pen and paper and asked the questioner for his name. His intent was probably benign. Rather than prolong this back-and-forth with just one person, he would write to him later. Nevertheless, a nervous hush fell over the room.

'Don't tell him, Pike,' someone whispered at my table and we all suppressed giggles.

John Birt was succeeded as DG by Greg Dyke. Greg and I had some history because he had almost given me my first job in broadcasting, back when he had been brought in to rescue the breakfast TV channel TV-AM and had announced in the press that he was looking for fresh talent on screen. I, having just won an intercollege public-speaking competition and feeling pretty chuffed with myself, had written to him and explained that I was just the boy he was looking for because I was as fresh as they came.

When I say he had *almost* given me my first job, I mean he wrote back to me on TV-AM stationery and I had that letter pinned on my wall for many years. This was more than just a standard rejection because he took the time to add the words, 'Frankly, I think you need a lot more experience.' Far from seeing that as a complete turn-down, I saw within those words a glimmer of hope.

When Greg Dyke became Director General there was a 'ring-main broadcast' – an internal screening of his first speech to the staff – staged at Television Centre in London but beamed to every BBC office across the country. It was instantly apparent that his style of leadership was going to be very different from John Birt. He spoke to us like a friend, like one of our best mates down the pub who, through some fluke or clerical error, had been handed the biggest job in British broadcasting. Once again it was someone from News who asked the tough question. Tony Blair was the Prime Minister at the time and it had been reported that Greg Dyke had donated cash to the Labour Party, and so his appointment was tainted with accusations of cronyism. So, what would he do, our News man asked, if Blair's spin doctor, Alistair Campbell, called him one morning to complain about a news story?

'I'd listen politely and thank him for his call and then get on with my day,' was the new DG's optimistic response. Little did we know how portentous that question and that answer would turn out to be.

If John Birt had been the black-and-white DG, Greg Dyke was all about colour. He embarked on a project designed to change the culture of the BBC which he labelled 'Making it Happen' and, probably because he was a big football fan, he supplied us with referee-style yellow cards emblazoned with the slogan 'Cut the Crap'. These, he explained, could be brandished at any meeting or in circumstances where it seemed like the mythical Programme Prevention Department was at work.

Unlike the austere *Extending Choice* gatherings, 'Making it Happen' sessions were held in huge rooms decorated to look like circus tents. We could sit on bean-bags and there would be bowls of sweets on the tables and a magician entertaining us before the serious agenda of the day got underway. Staff applauded when Greg described some of the nonsense he had encountered in his first few months. An oft-cited example concerned the cost of borrowing music CDs from the BBC Gramophone Library. Accountants had told the Library it must cover its own costs, so production departments were being charged more than £10 for every loan. This was despite the fact that anyone could wander down to Fopp or HMV and buy the same CD outright for a fiver. As a result, producers were creating their own collections and, if you walked into a music production office you would see stacks of CDs on every desk. Greg Dyke asked us to realise that we all worked for the same organisation.

'We are one BBC,' was his first mantra, 'and great things happen when we work together.'

Still, despite this new open, friendly and accessible style, his first visit to BBC Scotland created the usual sense of nervousness for the executives in Glasgow. We were told that 'Greg' wanted to wander casually through Queen Margaret Drive and chat to any random members of staff he came across. He didn't want anything too formal or stage-managed. So, some informality was carefully stage-managed. There was a fear that he might bump into the wrong people; he might meet some moaners from the Glasgow newsroom and hear that morale there was at rock bottom. That wouldn't do. So, as he wandered down the corridors, a number of senior managers were assigned to different floors so that they could report on where he been and whom he had spoken to. I'm sure he must have wondered why so many members of the BBC Scotland Executive Board were suddenly busy inspecting fire extinguishers and straightening framed publicity photographs.

The Dyke Era included my most enjoyable years as a programme-maker at the BBC and it really did feel as if anything was possible. Successes were celebrated and failures were treated as a necessary part of the creative process. 'You are allowed to fail,' Greg told us. 'Of course if you fail fifteen times in a row, we might start asking questions.'

At BBC Scotland there seemed to be more money available for programmes. A soap opera – *River City* – was launched from purpose-built studios in Dumbarton. BBC Scotland secured the rights to Scottish football on TV and radio. Comedies like *Chewin' the Fat* had migrated from radio to television and spawned spin-offs like *Still Game*. In radio there was a similar can-do spirt and there was investment in new programmes and outside broadcast vehicles for Radio Scotland.

The circus tents left town, of course, when the BBC became embroiled in a row with the Labour Government over the Iraq War Dossier. Conversations with spin doctor Alistair Campbell became public and hostile. When Greg Dyke offered his resignation to the Board of Governors it was – much to his surprise and the shock of the staff – accepted. The fun was over and a punishing licence-fee settlement would soon usher in a new era of cutbacks.

Next up was Mark Thompson. The former Head of BBC Nations and Regions was an old lunch companion of mine, by which I mean, in his former role he had instituted a series of 'get to know you' lunches at Broadcasting House in London, and every month or so a selection of mid- to low-level staff from across the UK were invited to chat with him for an hour – an exact hour – over soup and sandwiches. I had been to one of these.

Mark Thompson could turn on the charm and, in one-to-one conversations or with small groups, he gave the impression of being candid to the point of being indiscreet. On a visit to Inverness, he asked to speak to me alone before he addressed the rest of the staff. He wanted to know about the burning issues. I talked about the political situation, relationships with network radio and, almost as an afterthought, mentioned that there had been a leak in the roof over the weekend and people might ask about refurbishment plans for the building. When he talked to staff he managed, in a most impressive way, to punctuate his prepared speech with these little snippets of local relevance, and staff were quite astonished that the Director General of the BBC was so on the ball that he even knew about our leaking roof.

What really excited this DG, I suspect, was the international reputation of the BBC. In his chat with me he had talked about how the big American television networks were cutting back on international coverage and how the BBC might find an opportunity to fill the gap. I told him there was a similar situation here in the Highlands with Moray Firth Radio cutting its news output. He nodded. That evening, there was a dinner at a nearby restaurant and as we took our seats there was some small talk about how all management expenses claims had to be declared and made public, and how the risk of embarrassment in newspaper articles was leading more of us to pay for meals and travel out of our own pockets. In my case, I was talking about the odd taxi to a train station or a quick meal at Burger King. At the DG's level things were very different. He told us how a very famous international broadcaster had a habit of inviting him for lunch in expensive London restaurants and would always arrive first so as to order the most expensive bottle from the wine list. There would be some talk about a few programme ideas – all of them impractical – and then said broadcaster would make a half-hearted offer to pick up the bill. This had to be refused under new bribery rules and the bill was too high to be claimed back through expenses. I told the DG I was having exactly the same problem.

'Just picture a pint of Tennent's lager instead of fancy wine,' I said, 'and we could be living parallel lives.'

He nodded.

The only other DG I have encountered was the present incumbent, Lord Hall – Tony, of course. I've only met him twice, both times in Edinburgh during the festivals, when he toured the BBC's tented village up at Gillespie's School. It had taken years, but the BBC had finally seen the wisdom of concentrating its festival firepower in one location. The first year that Tony Hall visited he made a point of coming backstage at the theatre tent and shaking hands with presenters. The second year, he must have skipped some handshakes because presenters with fragile egos – or those with just a few months left on their contracts – began to wonder if this lack of flesh-pressing signalled their imminent demise. Such was the power of the DG to make an impression, unintentionally, with the things he didn't do.

Now, you may have noticed I have skipped a DG. Between Thompson and Hall there was a man I wish I had met because the one snippet of information I heard about him was that he was a stickler for punctuality. This, as former colleagues will tell you, is an obsession of mine because so many BBC meetings either start late or finish late, and it has a knock-on effect for the whole day as people straggle from one glass office to another. Staff finding a booked room occupied by a meeting that's over-running would linger at the door or press their faces against the glass like well-dressed zombies. This new DG, we heard, was going to change all that and I would happily have volunteered to be part of a time-keeping force, so long as there was a peaked hat and stopwatch included with the role. Alas, this new DG was George Entwistle, who was the biggest casualty of the Jimmy Savile scandal and its aftermath. After just sixty-seven days, his time was up.

10.

THE ELEPHANT IN THE ROOM

I'm a seventh son, but not of a seventh son. I have one older sister and six older brothers. At one time or another, five of those brothers were in the British Army, the Ordnance Corps. When asked why I had not enlisted alongside my brothers in arms, I explained that khaki was not my colour and the only military service that had ever tempted me was the RAF because blue went so much better with my eyes. I would also point out that military service carried with it the very real risk of being killed in action – not something I'm keen on.

Growing up in Easterhouse, many of my friends were tempted to join the military. You could put this down to a lack of other opportunities or else give credit to the Army for their PR efforts. Once a year they transformed the red-ash playing fields at the bottom of our street into a Forces fairground, displaying all manner of dazzling weaponry and sophisticated gadgetry. In a housing scheme bereft of amenities, the soldiers arrived to offer two weeks of entertainment that included marching bands and precision parachute drops. During the rest of the year, their efforts were nudged along by the local police, who often pointed violent teenagers towards the recruitment office as an alternative to a night in the cells, a day in court and perhaps a lifetime behind bars.

Norman Drummond had talked about the kids he had met as a young churchman and how they lacked aspiration and ambition. I wondered if BBC Scotland could deploy its know-how and expose a similar community to the range of experiences that only we could put together. I thought about all our different departments: Sport, Music, Comedy, Drama and the so-called backroom expertise of technicians, make-up artists, set designers, film editors and, yes, even our accountants. All had skills to offer. Imagine if we chose a single town and, for an entire year, week after week, we arranged for different groups of our staff to go there and talk to local teenagers about their work.

So was born the concept of *SoundTown* and, in the spirit of Greg Dyke's 'Making it Happen' initiative, colleagues across BBC Scotland and beyond were eager to help. We would choose a high school in one town and build a radio station in a spare classroom. Radio Scotland would benefit from this fixed link to the town, because we could ask children, teachers, parents and local townspeople to contribute to our various programmes. Asked why I wanted to stay in one place for a year, I explained the importance of establishing a real relationship with the people, rather than a whistle-stop tour of poverty hot spots.

We invited schools across Scotland to apply and for our first town we chose Dalmellington, a former mining community in East Ayrshire, which one pupil described to us as 'a place that people pass through on their way to somewhere more interesting'. We built our studio in Doon Academy and scheduled regular visits from different departments. We knew that the various aspects of our work would appeal to some and not others, but we hoped to find something for everyone. A live broadcast of *Off the Ball* with Tam Cowan and Stuart Cosgrove went down a storm, but so too did an afternoon concert by the BBC Scottish Symphony Orchestra.

We wanted to reach out beyond the school gates and when we discovered that Dalmellington, despite its small size, had five pubs, we linked them together for a grand pub quiz with questions posed and voiced by BBC stars and celebrities. Author and broadcaster Muriel Gray spoke to the school book group, our gardening show offered tips for local horticulturalists, and so on.

We made mistakes along the way too. An initial concert to launch the project had, unwittingly, been scheduled at the same time as a big European football match on the telly. The turnout was so poor that we were reduced to wandering the streets asking people if they would come in. Teenagers invited to make a documentary about high-school kids visiting from America included scenes of underage drinking with vivid sounds of vomiting. Parents and teachers were furious. But a year later, at our finale event, a fundraising fun run through the town attracted mass participation and local runners found themselves jogging alongside famous names from the world of showbiz and sport. *SoundTown* was hailed as a huge success, and we repeated the formula for four more years in four different schools.

BBC Scotland had undergone yet another management shake-up and, to the delight of staff, the position of Head of Radio had been restored. My old boss, Maggie Cunningham, was now at the helm. She had cut the ribbon to open our first *SoundTown* and with that Greg Dyke spirit sweeping the land, encouraged us to do even more to engage with communities across Scotland.

Gareth Hydes, now running our Radio Events team, worked with me on a format called *Let's Do the Show Right Here*. BBC presenters are always being asked to put in personal appearances at school fetes and village fundraisers, but what if we encouraged communities to stage some kind of fundraising show with the promise that we would, indeed, supply a guest star and perhaps a well-known compere? We, in turn, could tell the story of that community in a half-hour feature and explain to listeners why the funds were so badly needed. News anchor Jackie Bird presented the first series and compered shows across Scotland, always bringing another famous name to help boost ticket sales: Barbara Dickson sang her hit songs in Aberfeldy; magician Paul Daniels conspired with the audience in Brookfield, explaining that radio was such a great medium for magic and making an entire elephant disappear; *Taggart* star James MacPherson agreed to take the main role in a 'Whodunnit' written by a housewife in Grangemouth – the first draft of this particular murder mystery lacked the crucial element of an actual murder, because, she explained, none of the local cast wanted to spend the duration of the show playing a corpse; Nicholas Parsons came to Lockerbie for a stage version of *Just a Minute* and his old TV hit *Sale of the Century*. Afterwards he joined us in the bar to tell stories of his early days in the Clydeside shipyards and his Scottish accent was as good as that of Jay Leno.

Then came *Class Act* in which – many years before Jamie Oliver tried the same trick – we invited some famous names to become schoolteachers for a day and lend their knowledge and experience to school pupils across the country. The theatre impresario Cameron Mackintosh went to Golspie and told how he used to produce plays for his family at home and make them pay to watch. He had done the same thing at school, selling tickets in August for the Christmas Revue – a born producer. I still laugh out loud remembering another edition of *Class Act* in which comedy actress Karen Dunbar described one of her first auditions and how nerves almost got the better of her:

'Then I asked myself, what did I think was going to happen? What was the worst that could happen? They're not going to shoot me here. My life is not in danger. And they're not going to call the police. I can't be arrested. The worst that could happen is that they don't like me and I don't get the job. That's all.'

In that audition, she did get the job and has never looked back.

A six-parter called *Asking 4 U* was inspired by Sarah and Alan reaching the age when they were asking Anne and me all sorts of questions, up to and including the meaning of life. We invited primary schoolchildren to pose any question they liked to whoever they liked and we then set out on a quest to obtain and record the answers. Again, because it was for kids, lots of famous names took part: Gordon Ramsay, Sir Peter Maxwell Davies, Jack Vettriano, Ian Rankin, Lorraine Kelly, S Club 7, Atomic Kitten, among others. We fell foul of the Downing Street spin machine, however, when Gordon Brown, as Chancellor of the Exchequer, declined to take part. His spokesman barked down the phone to producer Jo De Silva, who passed him on to me. I got a Malcolm-Tucker-style earful for suggesting we would include the child's question and say on air we didn't get an answer. Taking Greg Dyke's advice, I thanked him for his call and got on with my day. The saddest question came from a wee boy called Stephen who directed his question to Glasgow City Council's Refuse Department: 'When my cat was dying, why did you take it away? Me and my family wanted to bury it.'

There was a whole other programme in that one.

In this period, which lasted three or four years, there was a genuine willingness to try new things, to get out of our old forbidding BBC buildings and make contact with our audiences. With the *Works Bus*, we mimicked the idea of team-building away-days and took groups of office and factory workers on a mystery tour. The secret destination would turn out to be somewhere like the Riding for the Disabled Centre, where our unsuspecting workers were required to muck out stables or assist a farrier. In another format we invited a group of car salesmen in to make their own radio show, assigning each of them a role of producer, presenter or researcher. I remember the salesmen arrived determined to dispense with all that wishy-washy BBC political correctness and 'tell it like it is'. Within a few hours, though, we seemed to have indoctrinated them so much that they ended up making a programme so balanced and fair-minded it was almost a parody.

For *Ageing with Attitude* we sent young reporter Lisa Summers to a BBC make-up artist, who aged her by forty years. We then paraded her around the streets of Glasgow so that she could experience a little of the prejudice endured by older people.

We loved making those programmes, but I remembered a phrase I picked up from a colleague in London: 'It's always showtime at the BBC.'

By this she meant that people in the BBC were always telling each other about their achievements and hoping to gain favour with the next tier of management. If you worked in television that was easy to do: you just showed the footage or the final programme. For those in radio, there was a risk of invisibility unless you could make the cover of *Ariel,* the BBC's staff newspaper. Gareth Hydes and I did just that as we were photographed wearing straw hats and silly grins for a front-page feature on *Let's Do the Show Right Here.*

On social media, people now use the phrase 'pictures, or it didn't happen'. Thinking ahead, therefore, I did something that was fairly unusual for a radio department at the time. I drained some money from my own bank account and bought a new mini digital video camera and tripod. It wasn't good enough to make telly programmes, but it would help us tell BBC bosses what we were up to. 'Making it Happen' was all very well, but showing them what we had made happen was just as important.

Failing that, there was another way to get noticed by the BBC's Director General. You could invite Greg Dyke to take part in a Radio Scotland programme and ask him this: 'Would you agree that the media, probably in general, is hideously white and middle-class?'

To which he replied: 'I think the BBC is hideously white. I wouldn't like to make that generalisation about the media overall. I think the BBC is a predominantly white organisation.'

The question had been posed by Anvar Kahn when presenting our weekly multicultural programme, *The Mix*. That phrase 'hideously white' has lived on, attaching itself to the BBC in any subsequent coverage of its diversity policies. It certainly caused a stir at the time, and, aside from the newspaper headlines, it brought renewed efforts to tackle the BBC's relationship with what was called 'hard-to-find' audiences in ethnic communities. Those audiences were not really that hard to find, as I discovered on a visit to the south side of Glasgow and to the studio of a community radio station called Awaz FM.

The people running Awaz had a pretty deep understanding of the Asian community in that part of the city but, like all community stations, were operating on a shoestring budget. That prompted me to suggest there might be mutual benefit in having closer links between Awaz and BBC Scotland. The idea provoked some sardonic smiles and I knew there was a joke I was not in on. It turned out that, in the space of a year, I was now the fourth BBC visitor to have come for a tour and make a similar suggestion – but nothing had ever come of it. To be honest, nothing much came of my visit either. Over the years, at various BBC meetings to discuss diversity, some well-intentioned colleague would mention that they had 'discovered' Awaz FM and had suggested some kind of partnership. I could only smile, imagining the reaction that offer had received.

My approach to tackling 'diversity' on radio could best be described as pragmatic and, at worst, mercenary. I took issue with the 'portrayal reports' that radio producers had been asked to complete after a live broadcast. Unless it was mentioned overtly in the programme, or perhaps hinted at by an accent, the ethnic origin of any contributor would be a mystery to the audience. Many guests were booked unseen and spoke from one of the dozens of remote studios the BBC had dotted across the country and around the world. Producers were reluctant to conclude a programme by interrogating a guest about their racial origins just so they could complete the paperwork. Some simply made it all up.

My view was that, as programme-makers, our main concern should be relevance of the content to the audiences and if we could improve that relevance by reflecting the diversity of that audience, then it was a no-brainer. So, much like I had done with our approach to *SoundTown* and *Let's Do the Show Right Here* everything we did should result in programme content and not be an end in itself.

With that in mind we created a new training initiative and recruited a small group of new researchers on to a Programme Diversity Team. The mission was to locate stories, topics and contributors that were not currently on the radar of the main news and speech strands. At times, our diversity researchers would be embedded within the main programme teams; at others they would work together as a unit on their own special projects. Stand-out talents such as Muslim Alim went on in later years to become a commissioning executive in television, and Laura McCrum made a beautiful documentary about visiting her extended family in Kenya, before going on to present our music show *Black Street*.

Our other main training initiative at that time was the Radio Scotland Production Trainee scheme. We chose six people from hundreds of applications and, like the diversity trainees, each was sent for periods of secondment at our bases around Scotland. Unbeknown to me at the time, they became known as 'The Zycinski Youth', although some, like Richard Melvin, had already worked at the music station Beat 106, and before that he had been a medical rep for Pfizer flogging the merits of a new wonder-drug called Viagra. I enjoyed leading those training initiatives, just as I still enjoy speaking to media students at colleges and universities. Broadcasting seems to be in a constant state of flux and it's true that the technology to make the programmes and the kit required to see or hear them, is forever evolving and improving. But at a fundamental level, I tell students, they need curiosity to find stories and the creativity to develop ideas. I worry that the multitude of hungry outlets requiring content skews the balance away from original journalism and towards information-processing, as stories are converted from print, to radio, to television, to online and now social media.

Journalists that I have met and admire include people like Eamonn O'Neill, who combines years of experience with an international network of contacts and ever-improving techniques in online research and investigation. Equally, a tabloid showbiz reporter like Bev Lyons can track down any celebrity visiting Scotland and has a network of 'superfans' who often call her when a famous visitor is spotted at an airport, hotel or nightclub. Both Eamonn and Bev in their own way know how to come up with the goods and find the story. For me, with my natural nosiness about people and their life stories, it's all about asking the right questions and listening, really listening, to the answers.

When students ask me about interview techniques, I tell them to imagine being on a long bus journey – Edinburgh to London, say – and sitting beside someone who seems reluctant to engage in small talk. I ask them to challenge themselves to persuade that fellow passenger to engage in meaningful conversation beyond chit-chat about the weather, speed of the bus or the blocked toilet. As soon as they can persuade the person to reveal something personal, no matter how trivial, then they should assume that the Freudian subconscious is at work and a file has been intentionally opened by the brain. Explore that file and they might open another file or even another three and, well before they know it, their hitherto shy seat companion is blabbering away. Somewhere in that blabber, they might find a story. There's also a pleasant side effect, because people will have a positive view of the conversation if they are left to do most of the talking – even if they don't realise that's what's happening. Afterwards they might go home and tell friends, 'I met this really interesting person on the bus. We had a great chat.'

'Oh really?' their friend will say. 'What was he/she saying?'

'Well, oh, I don't really remember, but they were great to talk to.'

I demonstrated this technique to the trainees by inventing a programme called *Life on the Bench*. My bet to them was that I could walk into any public park with a recording machine and, within an hour, come back with four interesting stories from complete strangers. To prove my point, I went over to the Botanic Gardens in Glasgow one lunchtime and, flashing my BBC ID card to prove I wasn't a complete lunatic, began conversations with people who, sitting on a bench, looked like they had time to talk. Once they were comfortable with my company, I asked if I could switch on my machine and record their stories for the radio. Within three quarters of an hour I had a story about a man who had been one of the first to climb the Berlin Wall, a widowed pensioner facing eviction, and the experiences of a young transgender teen. Back in the office, the trainees told me I had failed because I only had three stories instead of the promised four. I vowed to go back to the park the following day and complete the challenge.

Now, here's an odd thing, given all my babble about the subconscious. The night before I went back to the Botanic Gardens to get my fourth story, I had an upsetting dream that I was in the park when planes flew overhead dropping bombs and, as nearby buildings crumbled, I tried to take refuge in a bus shelter. At lunchtime the following day I was back in the real park and got talking to a young American student who told me that she was at the end of her four years in Glasgow and was now engaged to be married to her Scottish boyfriend. She told me she didn't want to settle in Scotland because the political situation, with George Bush then President of the United States, had made her a target for all sorts of anti-American comments, as if she were personally responsible for foreign policy. I thought her story was interesting with that bitter pay-off and I went back over to the BBC to tell the trainees. I was going up the stairs to the production office when a young researcher called Hermeet Chadha called to me over the bannister.

'Jeff, have you seen the news?'

'No, I've been out.'

'It's the Trade Centre in New York,' he said. 'A plane crashed into it and it's on fire. It's on the TV.'

And so it was. And then another plane hit the second tower. It was 11th September 2001. Soon, in Iraq and Afghanistan, our troops would be on the march. I wonder how many of them had been recruited from places like Easterhouse.

11.

BRAINWAVES

These days most people know what goes on behind the scenes in television. That's because TV people love making programmes about themselves. Think *Gogglebox* or *Telly Addicts*. We can all remember magazine shows on children's TV doing that thing where the presenter would walk off the set with the camera crew in tow and lead us, the viewers, down grubby corridors and into the gallery where the director and vision-mixer would be working on the very programme that we were watching at that moment. It messed with your head, like looking into one of those endless mirrors or – and I accept this is the devil in me coming to the fore – maybe it was a vivid illustration of TV people disappearing up their own back passage.

What they never told you on those programmes, though, was anything about the internal politics that went on within television companies. I'm not saying broadcasting is different from any other company or organisation in that regard, but maybe something weird happens when creative people are asked to soil their hands with the business of pitching ideas and beating their competitors to the next green-lit project. It's the money: unlike in radio, the sums of money in television can be so large you'd almost want to make a documentary about them. But there's where madness lies.

So, imagine me, a hitherto naive soul from the pure and innocent realm of radio, suddenly thrust into a sixth-floor conference room at the BBC's Television Centre in London. There I was, pitching a programme idea to the Controller of BBC 1. He was surrounded by his team of assistants, researchers and analysts, who would all take a view on whether my idea was worthy of the thousands of pounds he could send my way. How the heck did I get there and what the hell was I doing with a children's toy in my hands, and showing these very important executives how it worked? And why was it so important to the future of BBC 1?

It had started, as so many things did in television, with a glib phrase. In the 1990s, ITV had come up with a game show that, if the telly insiders of the time were to be believed, was so big that it would destroy all competitors and leave rival executives broken and sucking their thumbs in a padded cell. The show was called *Who Wants to be a Millionaire?* and thus, a new phrase was born: 'Beat *Millionaire*.'

Channel chiefs scrambled to find a format that could tempt viewers away from this new game show and, at the BBC, production departments around the UK were charged with coming up with ideas. At BBC Scotland, now in the throes of multi-platform production, I was among those who were asked to chip in some thoughts. This was the part of the job I most enjoyed: the ideas part. So, the first thing I did was to sit down and watch back-to-back episodes of the *Millionaire* show. It was gripping stuff and the only flaw I could see was that the early easy questions – where the contestants built their prize total from £100 to £1,000 – was a bit tedious and the viewer was impatient to get into the meaty stuff where the prize money at risk was in the tens of thousands of pounds. There was something else, and this led me back to my days studying psychology. In order to qualify for a place in the big-money seat opposite the presenter, Chris Tarrant, the competitors had to take part in a round called 'Fastest Finger First'. This involved looking at a question that had four correct answers and then, using the key pad in front of them, they had to put the answers in the correct order. In psychological or neurological terms this was a different challenge from the main round where they simply answered general knowledge questions. 'Fastest Finger First' involved knowledge, sequencing and motor skills. No wonder then that, at the time of our brainstorming, no one had actually won a million pounds on *Who Wants to be a Millionaire*? The fix, as I saw it, was in the format.

I was musing on this to the Head of Factual Programmes and suggesting that we should tap in to all the latest work that was being done in understanding the functions of the brain and maybe develop a format that allowed us to test different neurological strengths. Thus, *Brainwaves* was born, which I wrote up with suitable illustrations and footnotes, much as if I had been writing an academic paper back in my undergraduate days. The Head of Factual then took it to her boss, the Head of Production, but at some point her explanation floundered and, in an attempt to rescue the pitch, I was called in to explain it to the top TV people at BBC Scotland. I did so, illustrating how each round would tap into a different brain skill and pointing out the difference between that and the *Millionaire* format. I ended with a flourish: 'So, it stands to reason,' I said, concluding my tutorial, 'that the only person who could ever win £1 million on *Who Wants to be a Millionaire?* would be the BBC 1 *Brainwaves* champion.'

Much applause. Like a Vegas comedian after a good gig, I might have bowed and muttered something about being 'here all week' and 'try the veal'. I was so damn pleased with myself that I almost missed the Head of Production proclaiming that it should be me who should join him on the plane to London the following week and me who should sell the idea directly to the Controller of BBC 1.

'Sorry, what? Me?'

'Yes, you're the only one who understands this.'

'But–'

'So, that's decided then.'

The others moved on to talk about the list of proposals that would be pitched at that meeting: a mixture of new ideas and some existing programmes that they were hoping to be recommissioned. This is where the internal politics kicks in because my *Brainwaves* idea was quite far away from being a 'factual' offering. It might well be wrapped up in some fairly basic pseudo-science, but it was still a game show, and should have been born from the collective brains of the Entertainment Department. In my naivety I assumed that all the experienced telly people would now begin to tweak the format, add in those elements of jeopardy that seemed to be required and toss out some of my dull science bits. That way we might get to a proposal that had a chance of being commissioned.

Instead, a Development Executive spent the next week or so equipping me with an armoury of BBC-branded props and charts, all supplied by the Graphics Department. I had a glossy picture board showing the different bits of the brain and an adapted version of the children's toy, Simon; the one where you had to press four big buttons to repeat an ever-extending sequence of lights and sounds. All of this was to help illustrate different brain skills to those who were not as fortunate as I was to have remembered stuff from first-year psychology courses. It was also deemed necessary to get a quote from an actual neuroscientist who would back up my bold assertion that the brain had different areas of expertise. Such an expert was remarkably easy to find once we had mentioned the prospect of future involvement in a long-running and lucrative TV series.

There were six of us on that plane to London and as we filed into Television Centre, I had memories of all the programmes that had been made there: *The Multi-Coloured Swap Shop*, *Grandstand*, *Doctor Who*. On the sixth floor we entered a long room with windows on one side offering the uninspiring vista of Shepherd's Bush and White City. On the facing wall there was a sideboard laden with tea, coffee and cut fruit. There was always fruit at BBC meetings in those days. Perhaps it was felt that executives would suffer scurvy unless orange segments and grapes were provided at least twice a day.

The trouble began as we took our seats, with our backs to the window. As we settled there, waiting for the

Controller's people to arrive, the Head of Production turned to the Head of Entertainment.

'Don't we usually sit on the other side of the table?'

'No,' he responded with absolute certainty. 'We're always on this side.'

The Head of Production was doubtful. 'Hmmm.'

'Trust me. It's always this side for us. They like to be near the fruit.'

The jitters started when the BBC 1 team began to file in one by one and, as each researcher, scheduler and analyst walked in, they did a double-take as they noticed our seating positions.

'Oh, so you're on that side today? That makes a change.'

By the time the fourth member of their team had come in and made a similar observation, the Head of Production was staring at the Head of Entertainment with the kind of face that suggested he was lucky that none of those sixth-floor windows were open. In fact, the only person not to mention the radical table position was the Controller of BBC 1, who arrived, dressed casually in tie-less, open-necked shirt and jeans (the standard TV uniform) and simply greeted us with a smile and a 'hello' as he helped himself to satsuma pieces and sat down. We, from Scotland, breathed a sigh of relief and opened our folders as we began to talk through various offers and awaited the response from the boss. This did not go well.

The first series of a sitcom about an RAF station in Scotland was deemed not to have worked and the Head of Entertainment's promises to make radical changes to the scripts, actors and location didn't persuade the Controller, who put the final nail in the coffin when he mentioned that his own father had been in the RAF and found the show a little offensive. We turned the page.

Then there was a bizarre fracas about the weekly film show because the executive producer pointed out that the presenter wasn't happy with the after-midnight transmission time. The Controller got grumpy and said it was BBC Scotland's job to manage their talent and if we couldn't do that then well, maybe it was time to rethink our involvement in the show. We turned the page.

An idea about James Bond film scores was rejected on the grounds that ITV had basically sown up the Bond franchise and had rights to screen all the old films, so why get involved with that? We turned the page.

It went on like this until it came time to discuss *Brainwaves*. Despite the disappointments of the previous hour, the Head of Production managed a confident smile as he introduced me as 'Jeff Zycinski, the brains behind *Brainwaves*'. I cleared my throat.

'I think we're all sharing a brain here today.'

No idea why I said that. No idea at all.

I pressed on. I produced my lovely boards and charts, gave a mini-lecture on the history of neurology, pressed the buzzers on the Simon game for a little longer than was necessary and, sensing that everyone might now be in need of more fruit, brought my spiel to an end with the well-rehearsed line, 'So, according to our neuroscientist [not me, you notice] the only person who could win *Who Wants to be a Millionaire?* would be the BBC 1 *Brainwaves* champion.'

I paused. Everyone was smiling. The smiles on our side were fixed and nervous. The smiles on the other side were kindly and mildly pitying. I think they could see that I was out of my depth, like some poor innocent who had got involved with a bad crowd – the kind of stinkers who came up with Air Force sit-coms. The Controller thanked me then he asked one of his analysts for his thoughts. Said analyst consulted some paperwork in front of him and suggested that *Brainwaves* might get a decent audience if it started as a slow burner on BBC 2. A money man was asked if BBC Worldwide would be prepared to contribute any cash in return for international sales rights. That was a yes. The Controller then said he would fund a non-transmission pilot. Commercial confidentiality prevents me from disclosing the size of that fund, but the equivalent cash spent in radio would have paid for half a dozen documentaries. I was shocked and thrilled and, as we left the room, I got handshakes of congratulations from my boss and the Head of Production.

The Entertainment folk weren't quite so chuffed, but then, they had taken a bit of a battering. I felt for them and then, sitting on the plane on the way back to Glasgow, I wondered who they would ask to produce this pilot and whether I might have some minor involvement, perhaps researching the science bits.

It was worse than that. I was asked to oversee the whole thing and – again I think this is where internal politics might have played a part – no one from Entertainment wanted anything to do with it. I was teamed up with an experienced producer from BBC Scotland's Children's Department, Ed Gray, and then we got word that BBC 1 would be keen for Philippa Forrester to present the pilot.

Ed and I began working on contracting a set designer and recruiting contestants. This, as it turned out, was to be one of Ed's final projects as he had decided to leave the BBC because, as he put it, 'I don't understand it any more'. All was going well until we got a call from Philippa Forrester's agent saying she could no longer do the pilot. It turned out she was pregnant. We cast around for other ideas, each of which had to be approved by BBC 1. They expressed an interest in veteran newsman Peter Snow (he of the election night 'swingometer') and I duly gave him a call. He understood the idea immediately but wondered why we weren't linking the contestants' heads to some kind of apparatus that would show the different areas of the brain light up as they engaged in each task. The only piece of kit I could think might do this would be an MRI scanner, but I doubted whether we would get the loan of one from a local hospital given that they were using them for the wholly worthier task of diagnosing cancer patients. Of course, anyone could buy one outright for £2 million, but the budget for the pilot didn't quite stretch that far. Peter Snow declined.

We looked through recently submitted show reels from would-be presenters. Even as an editor in radio, I was often sent these video tapes, which consisted mainly of footage of beautiful and handsome young people talking to the camera; rarely did it show them doing anything as challenging as interviewing another person. It was all about looking good on screen and, yes, we needed a bit of that for *Brainwaves*. Another shortlist was sent to London and our enthusiasm coalesced around Isha Sesay, a young presenter with a degree from Cambridge under her belt. She subsequently won awards presenting news programmes on CNN International, but at that time had very little TV experience. Isha had warmth and enthusiasm as well as brains and she seemed genuinely interested in the show and making it a success.

By this time, we had agreed on a makeshift set for the pilot. Although on paper it had looked hi-tech and futuristic, in reality it resembled a 1970s disco with only the glitterball missing. We recorded a show with three contestants, each given a series of different brain challenges, but with no wires or electrodes attached to their heads. Sorry, Peter.

If you had watched television in the 1970s, you would probably have been way ahead of me here in seeing the big problem we had created for ourselves, but you have to understand how TV programmes are developed. Unlike radio, TV shows usually have a run of six, ten or thirteen shows, then it's a wrap and that production team is scattered and asked to work on something else until the next series goes into production. If a show fails, then work starts on developing ideas for the next pitching session. People on those teams tend to be young – I'm talking about people in their twenties and thirties – and their knowledge of television stems from ... well, watching television.

My friend Donald MacInnes, a producer/director, once observed how so many ideas were derivative and how TV people would often reference other shows to help explain their concepts.

'It's a bit like *Top of the Pops* mixed with *Ready, Steady, Cook!*' they might say, before adding the phrase, 'But not that.'

'It's a bit like *The Money Programme* combined with *The Generation Game* ... but not that.'

Cue nodding of heads and colleagues indicating they totally got it and it was awesome.

The trouble with *Brainwaves* was that it was also derivative, but rather than combining it with something else, we took something away. You could describe it thus: 'It's like *The Krypton Factor* ... that old 1970s game show, but minus the physical trials on the assault course. You know? The best bits?'

It was true. The challenges we devised to illustrate these different brain skills were reminiscent of *The Krypton Factor*: memory tests, moving blocks into a sequence, general knowledge and so forth. The only difference was that it all seemed to take place on an almost empty dance floor. Also there was no real element of jeopardy or strategy. Contestants couldn't undermine each other by, say, using a large mallet to rob an opponent of vital brain cells. We sent the pilot to London and awaited the verdict from the Controller. It was not green-lit, but not rejected. It was given the official status of 'amber'. As far as I know, has it still. Meanwhile, BBC 1 went ahead with an alternative format called *The Weakest Link* and it became an international hit. On ITV, several people won the top prize in *Who Wants to be a Millionaire?*

None of them, of course, were the BBC 1 *Brainwaves* champion.

12.

LOVE EVERYTHING

In 2004, towards the end of the summer, I was given a trial shot at running Radio Scotland. It had been at least five minutes since the last management restructure, but now Maggie Cunningham was to take up a new promoted post as Head of Programmes and Services; a three-day-a-week job-share with Donalda MacKinnon. Both would report to Ken MacQuarrie, who had stepped into John McCormick's job as Controller of BBC Scotland.

Kenny promptly locked himself in his office for three months to sort out the plans for Pacific Quay. The move to a new HQ across the river had been occupying a lot of our attention, and various workshops had been set up to hammer out new ways of working and discuss the technology that would be available to us. Before starting the original tender process for the architects, a session had been held so that each department head could offer a wish list to the prospective bidders. One by one we talked from a rostrum as teams from the various firms scribbled notes.

I mentioned my trip to KIRO in Seattle many moons ago and how the building there exuded excitement, with a helipad for the News chopper and satellite dishes on the roof. I asked that, internally, the building should be welcoming for visitors and, in contrast to Queen Margaret Drive, there should be no dark corridors and closed doors. I remembered getting a tour of the BBC's old Queen Street studios in Edinburgh. The Campus Editor had led me through a maze of narrow corridors, opening doors every now and then to reveal a production team responsible for a particular programme. On one such stop the open door revealed two startled producers.

'Oh, I forgot about these two,' said my guide, 'I thought we'd decommissioned that programme.'

I think he was joking.

In designing the building at Pacific Quay, I have no idea how much notice the architects took of our opinions. We did get glass walls and the satellite dishes, but no helipad. I think most would agree that the building is more impressive inside than out. The nearby Science Centre is shaped like an orange segment and the ridge-backed Clyde auditorium is referred to as 'the Armadillo'. The BBC building, on the other hand, looks to the casual observer like a simple glass block. It picked up many awards. but one cruel critic did describe it as looking like 'the box the Science Centre came in'.

As Kenny worked through his urgent to-do list for the new HQ, Maggie and Donalda made sure we were still actually making programmes. Within months they would find a new Head of Radio. In the meantime, I was the Acting Head.

I was keen to start making an impact and not simply because I needed to prove I would be up to the job in the longer term. In truth, I felt my chances of becoming Head of Radio permanently were at best 50/50, because I knew there would be other candidates with more years of service. The vacancy would also be open to external applicants and it was one of those jobs that would attract people from commercial radio because the title, unlike many other BBC positions, was fairly easy to understand. My main thought at that time, though, was that I might only have a small window of opportunity to take some actions and address the frustrations I felt about the way the station sounded.

To that end, I recruited the Hollywood actor Richard Dreyfuss to help me. Well, not exactly. It was actually an American radio consultant by the name of Dan O'Day, but to me he looked like the twin of the younger Dreyfuss and had the same self-confident Californian manner. I had gone to LA to attend one of Dan's three-day seminars and it was the first time I'd ever seen anyone take the things that I knew instinctively made good radio and offer them back to the delegates in a codified set of rules, hints, tips and warnings. Also, he was funny. I asked him to do two sessions – one in Glasgow and the other in Edinburgh – and they were almost like a Fringe show. He used his library of audio clips to illustrate the dos and don'ts, based on things he had heard, admired or cringed at from stations all over the world.

One example was that hackneyed feature the Birthday List, when a radio presenter gave a roll-call of famous people

– dead and alive – who might also be sharing a birthday with you on that day. The point of this, said Dan, was so that listeners could measure their own age and lifespan against a famous person and maybe mention to the people at work that, 'Hey, I'm younger than Tom Cruise', and feel they were not as near to the grave as they feared. But who, asked Dan, as he fired a clip of a bored presenter going through the motions, really wants to know that, 'also born on this day was notorious Nazi, Adolf Eichmann, responsible for implementing Hitler's Final Solution that led to the murder of millions of Jews'?

It was a fair point. You would have trouble shoe-horning that into the conversation at coffee break.

As the Acting Head, I wasn't in a position to introduce long-lasting changes, but I could make my mark on the Christmas schedule, so I set about eliciting ideas and offers from the different departments and the small group of independent producers who supplied programmes to Radio Scotland. Time flew and, at the end of November, the post of Head of Radio was advertised and it became known that as many as ten candidates would be interviewed. I was determined to put up a good show, but I was also philosophical about it. I was forty-one years old and considered that I was still young enough to miss out this time around and go for it again in a few years. There were also the prospects of more work in television, despite my fraught experiences with *Brainwaves* and the earlier lack of enthusiasm for BBC Choice.

There were four people on the interview panel: Kenny, Maggie, Donalda and the Head of Human Resources, Steve Ansell. I began with the five-slide PowerPoint presentation that had been requested and, fortunately, my months of shooting and editing video at our various outreach events came in useful. Whereas other candidates might have adorned their slides with text, clip art and the odd photograph, mine burst into life with sound and moving pictures which included a heartfelt message from one of the school kids at Doon Academy saying how much the *SoundTown* project had changed their lives. I also had clips of *VIP on Air*, a community station for blind and visually impaired listeners, that had been launched by Glasgow City Council and the RNIB. I had taken a position on the station's board, helped recruit the station manager and created BBC training opportunities for their staff and presenters. It had been an interesting experience with much debate as to whether this should be a general music station that just happened to be staffed by people with no or limited sight, or else a station that offered content directly relevant to such listeners. I argued for the latter in that visually impaired listeners, like all of us, had plenty of music stations to choose from and it would be the tailored content that would make *VIP on Air* different.

Pressed by the interview panel for an equivalent overall strategy for Radio Scotland, I resisted pointing to any genre which should be shut down. I argued that it was our place in Scotland and within Scottish culture that offered our unique selling point, and it would be foolish to specialise too far. I described a cartoon I had once seen in *Punch*, which showed a very sophisticated seaside shop called 'Simply Spades'. In the window was a sign with an arrow directing customers 300 yards along the road to another shop they might need called 'Just Buckets'. You can take specialisation too far was my point. Radio Scotland had to have confidence in the things it did well and do them even better. Reaching for an analogy, I drew a comparison with the success of Tesco. Sure, I said, Tie Rack sold ties and Thornton's sold toffee, but so did Tesco and it was no longer trying to be the best grocer in Britain, it was trying to be the best at everything it did.

I brought this back to the diversity of Radio Scotland's offering. I also mentioned a billboard campaign that was then running for *The Sun* newspaper: 'We know how you feel about football,' proclaimed one huge poster. 'We feel the same way.' Other posters in the campaign made similar statements about politics and showbiz gossip.

'Radio Scotland needs to love everything,' I argued, 'because there are sections of our audience who love the different things we do. But a well-run supermarket doesn't look like a jumble sale. Things have to be put in order, displayed well, subjected to quality control and marketed cleverly. It also helps if the checkout attendants aren't grumpy sods.' It also helps, I thought, if the staff on the fish counter don't openly badmouth their colleagues in the bakery section. As Greg Dyke had said: 'Great things happen when we work together'.

The interview lasted more than an hour and there were times when I found myself waffling. For a few minutes, my mention of Tie Rack led us all down a cul-de-sac about Sock Shop, but we got back on track. At the end I was given the usual opportunity to ask questions of the panel, but I could see they were already pushed for time, so I kept it light.

'I just want to apologise for one thing,' I said.

They looked at me waiting.

'This haircut,' I said. 'I left it to the last minute and there was only one place open. I know it's pretty brutal.'

'We didn't like to say,' said Donalda.

A few more smiles and thank yous and I was out of the room, breathing hard and regretting, as everyone does, all the brilliant things I had forgotten to say. Now all I had to do was await the decision. At the end of any BBC interview, all the candidates are told they might not hear about a decision for a day or two. This was usually a fib, but it was designed to give the panel a bit of breathing space in case there were issues to be resolved or the successful candidate haggled too long about a salary hike. In most cases, if you'd got the job, you'd get a call that night or, at worst, the following morning.

At home that evening, Anne had a bottle of Cava chilling in the fridge. Her confidence in me was higher than my own. Sarah and Alan, somewhat mystified by all these weeks of discussions about 'the big job', only knew that something fun might be happening. Never mind that bottle of fizzy stuff for Mummy and Daddy, Alan had also spotted a big chocolate cake in the fridge too. With each passing hour, Anne and I speculated as to what might be happening. We calculated the final candidate would be seen by 5 p.m., so, allowing for a tea and toilet break, they might start the discussion at half past five. Give them an hour or so to talk through those ten applications and we assumed they'd have a decision by seven at the latest. The phone might ring then.

By eight o'clock there had been no call, the kids were in bed and the bubbly and cake were still chilling.

Next day, I was in my office, unable to focus on anything. By home time, still no word, but Alan had been allowed cake anyway. No calls again that night and, in the office next morning, I started to pen a few words to my own team in which I admitted my disappointment but thanked them for their support and urged them to get behind the new Head of Radio. I was scratching my head to come up with a pithy final sentence when there was a knock on my door and Maggie Cunningham entered. Her expression was downcast as she sat on the chair opposite me.

'I'm sorry,' she began, 'there was a bit of a delay because Kenny was called to meetings in London and we couldn't find time to get the panel back together for a decision.'

'That's okay,' I said.

'But we finished that discussion today and I just wanted to give you the news myself.'

'Thanks.'

'You are the new Head of Radio.'

I was speechless, delighted, tearful. My head was a jumble of different thoughts and emotions.

I called Anne with the good news. She screamed; happiness and relief. The tension had been unbearable. She told the kids.

Alan asked if this meant there would be another cake.

13.

BURSTING WITH NEW VARIETIES

When you take over the running of a radio station – much like if you take charge of any business – you need to have a good look at the books to find out how much cash is coming in and how much is going out. If you want to survive and prosper you need to work out what your customers – in this case, the audience – actually like about what you are offering and what else you can give them in future.

At the BBC, attempts to solve the mystery of how much things actually cost had been part and parcel of the *Producer Choice* project and that, in turn, had led to an influx of accountants, analysts and business managers, dismissed by production staff, naturally, as 'the bean counters'. Suspicion of these newcomers turned quickly to resentment when word spread that they were being accommodated in freshly painted offices with brand-new desks and computers. Worst of all, they had fancy new office chairs with padded seats. I don't know why those chairs caused so much consternation, but the quality of a department's office furniture did tend to signal their perceived value to the leadership of an organisation.

At Queen Margaret Drive, BBC Scotland's programme-makers were housed in an ever-expanding labyrinth of corridors, Portakabins and duplex extensions, whereas producers made do with a ramshackle collection of desks and chairs that had been gathering since the mid-1970s.

Along with the bean counters came, supposedly, new financial rigour: gone was the Wages Office offering cash advances to the unexpectedly skint, and new procurement procedures demanded a degree of scrutiny and approval before anyone bought the things they might need to keep a show on the road or an office ticking over. The days of buying a new Hoover from a petty-cash fund were over. Of course, people did find workarounds to all of these. When one team found that their trusty electric kettle had boiled its last litre, no one was prepared to fill out forms and go thirsty until permission came through to order a new one. Instead there was a furtive trip to Woolworths and reimbursement achieved through a quick payment to a fictitious freelancer called 'Mr A. Kettle'.

My predecessor as Head of Radio, Maggie Cunningham, was forever expressing frustration at the tightening of purse strings around Radio Scotland, but she had a courageous policy of 'better to seek forgiveness than permission', as she commissioned good ideas as and when she saw them. Admittedly, when it came to understanding the budget for radio, she had good reason to doubt how the sums had been worked out. The licence-fee money made its way from London to Glasgow, and thereafter it was shared out between Television and Radio, with a slice of those budgets subtracted to pay for news and sport. When you asked how those various figures had been calculated the answer usually came with smiles and shrugs. The split between Production and Broadcast complicated things further and the cynical term for all these transactions was called 'playing at shops'. For an organisation that didn't have to sell advertising to earn a crust, it certainly made heavy work of its financial planning.

My first move when appointed as Head of Radio was to gather all the money people into one room so that together, in a spirit of openness and collaboration, we could work out exactly how much I had to spend on programmes. This quest became more pressing when word came down from on high that, on top of the apparent overspend that radio was already carrying, we would have to save an additional £1 million as part of the BBC's Continuous Improvement process. As I waited for the various accountants and business managers to arrive, I realised I'd booked too small a meeting room, and by the time we were ready to begin, there were a dozen people all claiming to have a relationship of some kind with radio's budget. That in itself explained some of the problem.

Now, let me try and make this meeting of accountants sound a little more thrilling by asking you to imagine that scene in the film *Apollo 13*; the one where the astronauts are stranded in space and so the head of NASA Flight Control brings together all the relevant engineers and mathematicians to plan a rescue.

'Failure is not an option,' he warns them and that's exactly how I felt at my meeting. With ink markers and wipe boards, we worked through sum after sum. I think people could see I was as sincere about saving money as I was in spending it and we really did pull together.

'This is good,' I kept saying. 'I think we're getting there.'

By the end of the afternoon we had identified our true 'cost base', and even I was bandying about terms like 'WiP carried forward' and 'capital depreciation'. By mid-afternoon, we had a result and there were smiles and a ripple of applause. Not quite the whoops and back-slapping you'd see at Mission Control, but close. Then someone noticed that we'd double-counted one of the figures, so we started all over again, but we got there eventually.

Having got a grip on the budget, I now split our management team into a business group and a creative group. For the latter, I invited senior producers to sit alongside department editors as we discussed programme ideas. I wanted more brains around the table and I didn't want good ideas to be shouted down by an accountant worrying about the costs – we could sort that out at the other meeting.

When talking to the wider staff, though, I literally threw some cash on the table – £126.50 to be exact. Back then that was the annual licence fee and I thought it was important we all remembered who was paying our wages and what that amount of money might mean to many of our viewers and listeners.

Next came the fun part: choosing new programmes. Although we commissioned audience research and waited for the results, I was keen to use the summer schedule for a period of experimentation. This wasn't as impatient as it sounds because audience research could only tell you so much. Listeners knew what and who they liked and didn't like, because they could hear it on the air, but it was more difficult to get meaningful opinions about the ideas we had for the future unless we could find a way to demonstrate them.

I had already been talking to the staff about what we needed to do to modernise the schedule. Always keen on an analogy from the real world, I talked to them about Lucozade. The famous glucose drink had been around since the 1920s and, in its tall bottles needlessly wrapped in amber cellophane, had become the staple gift of hospital visitors, or the sticky brew you poured down the throat of ailing relatives – presumably in the hope that they would burp their way back to full health. Its image was old-fashioned and worthy, I said, but look at *this*.

Like a table magician, I now produced the smaller-sized bottle of Lucozade Sport and described how the company (now in Japanese hands incidentally) had changed the image of the drink so that Lucozade could find a new customer base of amateur athletes and joggers. For Radio Scotland to do the same, I said, we needed to do a lot more than just change the packaging; we needed some new ingredients in the mix too. I announced that some of our programmes would be taking a ten-week break over the summer months and hoped the teams who made them would see this as an opportunity to flex their creative muscles, try some new formats and allow our existing on-air talent to explore different interests.

On the faces in front of me I could see a mix of expressions: some looked excited by the prospect; others fearful; and a few just bored and sceptical. But the ideas soon started to come my way.

Tam Cowan – then known only for his funny football chat on Saturday afternoons – suggested a short series on 'crooners', and interviewed heroes such as Jack Jones, Neil Sedaka and Engelbert Humperdinck. Jackie Bird, familiar to Scottish audiences from *Reporting Scotland*, began writing a six-part sitcom, *Having it All*. Our music team created a new 'Does-what-it-says-on-the-tin' programme, *The Jazz House*, and, in Aberdeen, Bryan Burnett hosted an unusual request show in which listeners had to choose tracks built around a given theme. This became *Get It On* and offered a natural bridge between our daytime speech output and the specialist music shows in the evening. Our radio drama team who had established a reputation for adapting classic books for Radio 4, including Sherlock Holmes, now returned to Radio Scotland, starting with a contemporary play, *King of Hearts*, centred on the rivalry between the two big Edinburgh football clubs and the Russian ownership at Tynecastle. When I asked Drama Editor, Bruce Young, to provide me with photographs of the cast (something that's now a requirement for BBC iPlayer), he questioned my familiarity with the non-visual nature of the genre – 'You do know this is radio?' he asked.

A similar plea for new ideas having been made to independent producers, they too were soon knocking at my door. From the Comedy Unit, producer Gus Beattie persuaded the third star of *Chewin' the Fat*, Karen Dunbar, to host a mid-morning format called *Summer Supplement*. Regular posse guests on that show included relative newcomers such as Kevin Bridges and Susan Calman. Nick Lowe at Demus offered a new sketch comedy show called *Sabotage*. Richard Melvin's fledgling Dabster company began to build relationships with artists in America, including Dean Friedman and the New York based singer-songwriter-poet Lach, who had worked with the likes of Suzanne Vega.

By the time summer came, we counted forty new elements to the schedule and that became the basis of a colourful publicity campaign entitled 'Bursting with New Varieties'. BBC Scotland's marketing team did us proud with a batch of radio and television promos which, on BBC 1 and BBC 2 included a glossy animation sequence in which the changes to the schedule were represented as the growth of an exotic garden, and the new programmes were portrayed as plants and flowers, with their titles translated into mock Latin. It was exactly the message we wanted to convey: growth, creativity and fun. And by the time autumn kicked in and the football season restarted, we knew exactly which ideas had worked (or were affordable) and could become a permanent feature of the schedule. Others would be quietly jettisoned with no sense of a failure or a U-turn because these, after all, had just been 'summer fillers'.

The findings from our audience research now came in and included verbatim comments from focus groups. A mix of listeners and non-listeners had been invited to talk about Radio Scotland, while we in the management team listened and watched from behind a one-way mirror. Not much of what we heard surprised us. The station had just a handful of presenters who were well known: those who also had a television career.

Listeners who already liked the station tended to focus on one or two of their favourite presenters and drift away when other programmes came on air. Non-listeners were surprised and positive about the range of programmes offered by the station, but nothing they said convinced me that we could wrest them away from the regular habits or their love of big names like Terry Wogan and Ken Bruce on Radio 2. Wogan's popularity was unquestioned, but I knew from friends in commercial radio that it was Ken Bruce who, under the radar, was giving them a beating mid-morning.

All agreed though that Radio Scotland came in to its own when offering news and information in times of crisis or tragedy, such as severe winter weather or an emergency in the North Sea. Remembering the station's response to the Dunblane shooting, I made it a standing rule that, for breaking stories, News had absolute authority to interrupt the schedule and either extend bulletins or offer continuous coverage. No one needed to call me and get me out of a pub or bathtub for permission.

In summary, the audience research suggested we needed to do more to keep existing listeners tuned in for longer, and that we needed presenters who could offer a more personal wrap-around for the schedule. Music programmes that covered specific genres had a clear sense of purpose, but the remit of our speech programmes tended to blur and overlap with each other, meaning that listeners could often hear similar topics dealt with in the same way, hour after hour. I drew up clear briefs for these strands so that producers would know which angles they could pursue on any given story. I wanted a connection and flow between programmes, not duplication.

One thing we had to overcome immediately was the sense that each programme in the schedule was separate from the one before, or the one that followed. Presenters of the morning news programme, *Good Morning Scotland*, were particular guilty of 'closing down' the station, as they signed off each morning with phrases such as 'That's all from us. We'll be back at six tomorrow', without even a nod to the great things coming up after the nine o'clock junction, and sometimes not even a mention of the next news programme in the schedule at lunchtime.

Each programme also tended to have its own signature tune. As a senior producer in Inverness, I had been as guilty of this as anyone when I commissioned a theme for Tom Morton's programme, which had contained screaming guitars and the roar of motorbikes. What the Bat-out-of-Hell had I been thinking?

I then asked the presenters to join me, without their producers in tow, to discuss how we could sound more joined-up, more like a family. This time my analogy was less successful as I talked about my childhood love of superhero comics. I loved *Spiderman*, I told them, and I loved *The Fantastic Four*. But the first time I saw both feature in the same story I realised that they lived in the same universe and in fact the same city, and suddenly they all seemed so much more real.

The blank faces staring back at me made me realise I hadn't hit the mark – probably too many *Batman* fans in the room – so I had to spell it out.

'You all work for the same station,' I said, 'and we need you to sound as if you actually know and like each other. I want listeners to get the impression that you listen and look forward to each other's programmes. I need you to trail ahead to the next hour of the schedule, to talk to each other on air, and sound excited about the programmes and events that the station is trying to promote. Those promos and trails that Ken Lindsay makes? You need to play them, own them and not make them sound like they're a bit of a nuisance.'

Those who had worked in commercial radio or at a station such as BBC 5 Live – like Bryan Burnett and Gary Robertson – knew exactly what I was talking about; others were diverted by the thought of a party, and of actually socialising together instead of just pretending. One or two remained aloof and cynical. Richard Holloway, the former bishop who presented our Sunday morning programme, made the point that the presenters would actually need some written brief or script to be able to talk up the station's priorities. He phrased this in almost theological terms – 'We need a guiding intelligence' – and I suppose he was right.

Richard's input led me to create *The Daily Push*; a cheat-sheet for presenters that would, day by day, tell them what was coming up in the schedule, written in a way designed to make them sound as authentic as possible in their enthusiasm. We also introduced some cross-trailing of presenters on air so that there would be small chats between each of them in an effort to pull the audience through the news junctions and prevent our news sting acting like a Pavlovian cue to switch off. Eventually, although this took more time than I'd expected, I asked Ken Lindsay to commission a new set of station idents, stings and music beds, so the station would have a consistent identity. I talked about the McDonald's 'I'm loving it' adverts, and how, after establishing that slogan, they had stopped using the words that went with the tune so that consumers would hear the music and almost sing the slogan for themselves.

Every reference to the station on air would now be to 'BBC Radio Scotland'. Using the 'BBC' prefix was important in the world of online search engines and 'Radio Scotland' had been the name of an old pirate station in the 1960s. Also, the Scottish version of Real Radio, which had been launched with a stated intention to 'Rip the liver out of the BBC' – charming! – sometimes referred to itself as 'Real Radio Scotland'. BBC Radio Scotland, that eight-syllable phrase, would be replicated by eight notes in the new station sting: B–B–C–Ray–De–O–Scot–Land.

Still there were things I had little or no power to change. News programmes still fell under the control of the Head of News and the BBC's News Directorate. Sure, I could make suggestions about on-air talent and presentation techniques, but it would be up to the Head of News to decide whether or not to take such suggestions on board and to allocate the staffing and resources for the various programmes. The radio news teams were as confused about this as I was frustrated, and from time to time they would send me emails demanding change. Ruth Davidson, who became leader of the Conservative Party in Scotland, was then a brilliant presenter of Radio Scotland's' *Newsdrive* show. She came to see me soon after I was appointed Head of Radio and had a list of … well … *constructive* criticisms. As she put it, I was now 'about to play with the train set', so here were some of the things that needed fixing. As much as I agreed with many of her points, all I could do was pass them on to the Head of News and hope they would make it on to his to-do list.

In a staff survey, year after year, the biggest complaint centred around a lack of feedback and the alleged invisibility of senior managers. The latter was doubtless prompted by the amount of time we senior managers found ourselves closeted away in meeting rooms discussing the staff survey and working out how to make ourselves more visible. I began a round of meetings in Glasgow and started a regular circuit of our main production centres in Edinburgh, Aberdeen and Inverness.

I had promised staff that I wouldn't be tied to my office in Glasgow and, quite soon after my appointment, there came a chance to make good on that. The abandonment of the Campus Editor structure and then the further thinning of the management team in Aberdeen had resulted unintentionally in all of BBC Scotland's senior managers being located in Glasgow. When staff asked about this, Ken MacQuarrie said that he would be happy if any of those managers wanted to relocate to one of the other main centres. I discussed this with Anne and she was excited about a move back to Inverness. I was making the regular journey around Scotland in any case, so I reasoned it would make little difference if I started that trip in Inverness instead of Glasgow. Also, it would mean there would be a figure on the BBC Scotland Executive Board who would have a non-Central-Belt perspective and, in simple terms, read newspapers other than *The Scotsman* and *The Herald*, and who talked about football teams other than Celtic and Rangers.

My request was submitted, considered, referred upwards, referred downwards, reconsidered, and finally approved. By the summer of 2006, I was heading north with Anne, Sarah and Alan, to an Inverness that had now gained city status and was touting itself as 'the fastest-growing city in Europe'. Our children had imposed some tough conditions before agreeing to leave their school friends behind: Alan had demanded an elevated bed and a new PlayStation games console; Sarah had insisted on a puppy. Knowing that I was allergic to some breeds of dog, I began a bizarre testing process. Friends and neighbours were asked to bring their pets along to the house so that I could stick my face into their fur. So long as I didn't start itching and wheezing, that breed could be added to the shortlist for consideration. In the end we chose a honey-coloured Lhasa Apso, and Sarah named him 'Rascal'.

I started a weekly newsletter to keep production staff informed about my whereabouts and to offer praise and feedback on recent output, and I launched an external blog via BBC Online, aimed at connecting with listeners, although most of the feedback I received from the blog came when I reflected on happenings in my own family life and the antics of Sarah and Alan, whose identity I disguised as 'The Zedettes'. One exception was my description of an unusually fiery meeting to discuss whether we needed a dedicated programme for pet owners. As I said in the blog, when radio folk gather for a BBC meeting, you can usually expect things to be civilised. Raised voices are rare and verbal abuse is delivered with such coded eloquence that you can be insulted on a Monday but it will still be Friday before it dawns on you. ('Guiding intelligence'? Now I get it!) At one of our fortnightly creative meetings I handed out a sheet of statistics showing that forty per cent of Scottish households owned either a cat or a dog. There were about a dozen people at that meeting and until that point we had been united in a common purpose: to dedicate our lives to the service of public broadcasting.

But then it all kicked off.

The cat owners rounded on the dog owners. The pet-haters formed a breakaway faction. A senior colleague launched into a spiteful diatribe about her son's pet terrapin. Another threatened to tear up the handout, saying he didn't need facts and figures to tell him stuff he already knew. Cats were just evil, said another, and would happily kill us if they could organise themselves. Every utterance was greeted with either cheers, boos, gasps or sighs. I loved it and wished that every meeting could be imbued with such passion.

In the middle of June I tried to inject some fun and energy into our planning for the Christmas schedule. With the help and enthusiasm of producer Lizzy Clark, we commandeered one of the big meeting rooms, decorated it with fairy lights and asked programme-makers to ignore the early summer sunshine and immerse themselves in the festive spirit. The best ideas would be rewarded with a gift from Santa, played by Yours Truly. It was a bit silly, but it did help us design a festive schedule that was more than just the usual 'best of' compilations.

Back in the real world, we now awaited the verdict from listeners. Would any of our efforts have made a difference? The official RAJAR (Radio Joint Audience Research) figures always have a three-month time lag, but by the time the Scottish school holidays were over and the football season was about to kick off, the BBC Scotland Press Office was able to announce the following:

> BBC Radio Scotland continues to deliver growing audience figures.
>
> Reach, at 23.5 per cent, or 982,000 listeners, is up by 35,000 quarter on quarter, and by 134,000 year on year;
>
> Both share, at 10.3 per cent, and hours of listening, at 8.4 hours, are the highest they've been since the new RAJAR methodology began in 1999.
>
> Radio Scotland has also stayed ahead of BBC Radio 2 as the most listened-to station in Scotland.

Compared with the previous year, the station had gained more than 100,000 listeners, and though I later learned to treat RAJAR figures as more indicative of trends than specifics, it was an incredible leap and, frankly, a cause for relief as much as celebration. It was still short of my hoped-for target of a million listeners a week, but the straight-shooters in our research team – people who never let a good story get in the way of the truth – told me that, given the margin of error, we were in touching distance of that million.

Besides, there was more good news to come, with a clutch of nominations for that year's Sony Radio Academy Awards – known to all as 'the Sonys' – including one for me as 'Station Programmer of the Year'. These awards had become a big deal, culminating in a glitzy ceremony at the Grosvenor House Hotel in London. It usually began in good form, everyone dressed in designer gowns and dinner jackets, and a spirit of good humour and nervous optimism pervaded the huge ballroom. As the night progressed, however, and the balance of the room tipped in favour of people who hadn't won a damn thing, alcohol-fuelled bitterness seeped in. I have seen grown men brandish breadsticks to spear rivals on adjacent tables. Before joining colleagues at the Radio Scotland table, I had been tipped off that I hadn't won the big prize and so, as disappointing as that was, I could now relax, enjoy myself, knock back the wine and enjoy the success of our other winners.

But then came a low blow from the Academy supremo John Bradford as he took to the stage to reveal the winner.

'They warned me,' he said, 'that I would never be able to pronounce this winner's name ...'

All eyes were on me – the man with the hard-to-pronounce surname. Had I won the thing after all? Surely not. I didn't even have a speech prepared, plus there was now that blot of red wine on my double-cuffed shirt and my bow tie was round the back of my neck.

'But I'm going to make an attempt,' Bradford continued, 'And the winner is ... Richard Park!'

Doctor Dick, now guiding Capital Radio to the heights of glory, had come back to haunt me.

As I watched John Bradford hand him his prize, I retained my dignity, sharpened a breadstick and commented that there was more than one Dick on that stage.

Awards are great things when you win them, but when you don't, it's obligatory to denounce them as meaningless baubles, which are simply not as important as good listener numbers. Happily, we were able to take comfort in the next set of RAJAR figures and then the one after that, as the station audience soared to one million listeners a week and then, as I marked my first full year as Head of Radio, it hit 1,096,000.

Still, that meaningless bauble would have looked nice on my mantelpiece!

14.

MAKING HEADLINES

Despite these early successes, there was no shortage of critical press stories about the station, and the inevitable accusations of 'dumbing down' from those who seemed to think that what was really needed was a 'Radio 4 for Scotland'. This ignored the fact that Radio 4 already existed, was available all over Scotland and was expected to offer programmes of relevance to the whole of the UK. Nevertheless, I had sympathy for the view that Radio 4's arts coverage, for instance, rarely covered any cultural happenings beyond the M25. There was a rumour that London-based programme-makers would not travel north unless the job could be managed as a return trip within office hours, and besides, they all came up to Scotland for the Edinburgh Festivals so surely that was Scotland covered? Well, no.

Those who were most sniffy about Radio Scotland would dismiss the entire output as nothing but football and phone-ins. On Saturday afternoons, *Sportsound* was the biggest show in town, with only Radio Clyde's *Superscoreboard* programme offering any kind of competition. I was a staunch defender of phone-in formats if they offered journalistic value. A discussion about hospital waiting times or NHS cuts was given added depth if an actual doctor or nurse called in to describe conditions on the ground. Nor did I mind hearing Glasgow's taxi drivers give thoughts on potholes and traffic-management plans. I was less impressed with their views on geopolitics, but some days the news agenda dictated the choice of topics up for discussion.

I felt that those who complained about the popularity of football shows or formats that allowed for public opinion were actually insulting our listeners as much as they were our choices as programmers. I was happy to respond to critical press articles and avoided the temptation to inflame matters by pointing out that editors telling us how to run a radio station were presiding over steep and monthly declines in the sales of their newspapers. That would have been mean.

Once or twice I found myself at loggerheads with our own Press Office. A conversation format produced by our Inverness team was conceived around the notion of inviting imaginary guests to a dinner party. Vicky Featherstone, the bright and brilliant director of the new National Theatre of Scotland, offered a guest wish list that included the child killer Myra Hindley. I queried it with the producer on grounds of taste but was told that Vicky had already recorded the programme and had made a sound and intelligent case for her inclusion. To block the programme would risk accusations of censorship. I gave it the go-ahead and informed our Press Office, who issued some advance copies of the programme to reviewers. That's when things blew up.

When the tabloids got wind of Vicky's choices, she herself began to get cold feet. The National Theatre is funded by the Scottish Government and I suspect some of her second thoughts were prompted by queries from friends and funders. She asked the producer to cancel the programme and they, in turn, referred the matter to me. With just days to go before transmission, I pondered the matter. At the outset I had thought Myra Hindley had been a bad choice, even for a make-believe suggestion. The producer, who might have blocked it at the start, seemed ambivalent about the programme's transmission. Now that Vicky Featherstone had changed her mind who, I wondered, actually wanted this programme to be broadcast? I gave her a call and told her that we'd pull it. She suffered some damage from the press previews but was relieved that her fictional sit-down dinner with a psychopath would not be aired.

The BBC Scotland Press Office was not happy with my decision because they felt it reflected badly on them and showed an element of indecisiveness in our editorial choices. I could only apologise. I was also sorry that I hadn't been able to build a better relationship with the National Theatre; their choice of premises in the Bridge Arts Centre in Easterhouse had signalled a switch away from traditional thinking, and I had hoped Radio Scotland could have partnered with Vicky and her team on future projects.

Other headlines in those early days involved Lesley Riddoch. Frustrated by, among other things, the internal bureaucracy at the BBC, Lesley had quit her lunchtime phone-in show, but had hoped to bring it back as an independent producer, broadcasting it from her own studio in Dundee. I liked Lesley and was sorry she was no longer on air, but I was nervous about handing over ten hours of airtime every week to an indie with an unknown production team and untested technical facilities. In the end we compromised on a weekly show from Dundee, produced, as it happened, by Richard Melvin, who Lesley had seconded from his fledgling company Dabster Productions.

In the midst of all the press attention about Lesley's future with the BBC, the one thing I couldn't reveal was that, with budget cuts looming from London and job losses likely, I wasn't in a position to outsource so much output. Even when an independent production company offered to make a programme cheaper than it would cost in-house (as they always do), the sums didn't really add up because the BBC was still paying for the internal resources and also, because redundancy processes took so long, it would have still been paying the wages bill of the staff who were no longer required.

Having worried about the censorship issues with the dinner-party programme, I suddenly found myself accused of bowing to Islamic fundamentalism. I had been introduced to the angst-ridden writings of Franz Kafka back when I listened to Radio Prague, so the idea of a comedy show entitled *The Franz Kafka Big Band* made me laugh out loud, and it remains one of my favourite commissions. It was a surreal sketch show in which the writers, performers and producers, led by Colin Edwards and Innes Smith, really understood the medium. It was like cartoons on the radio: we heard how walnuts came to life and played tiny musical instruments, but could only be silenced by shotgun fire; the Apollo space missions were described as a mission to find the best sound for a rocket blast; the advert for a relaxation tape included the not-so-soothing voice of the late Ulster politician Ian Paisley ('You WILL relax!'). I loved it, but the Kafka team's humour led them into territory which, try as I might, I couldn't justify for the lunchtime slot on Saturday mornings. Killer sex robots anyone? I was loath to leave any of their work unheard, so we created an additional evening slot for an edgier version of the show.

Never fearful of biting the hand that fed them, a recurring character was an idiotic figure known as the 'Head of Radio Scotland', who drove his little open-topped car to his office every day for pointless meetings. The truth hurt. The series was produced under the banner of Nick Lowe's Demus Productions, but a second series was delivered too close to the scheduled transmission date, and I felt the material was not as strong nor as funny as the original, and delayed broadcasting it so they could have another crack at it. This, in turn, led to UK-wide press stories – and even a cartoon in *The Guardian* – about the BBC fearing reprisals because there was a sketch about Rolf Harris painting a picture of the Prophet Mohammed.

It was difficult to respond to those stories without saying that it was more about lack of funniness rather than political correctness. I didn't want to trash the talent. A few years later, I had hoped to revive *The Franz Kafka Big Band*, and asked Nick to get the band back together to deliver a compilation of the old sketches, as well as a one-off original show. The compilation was as funny as I remembered, but the new show was an odd James Bond spoof, in which the Head of Radio Scotland was blown to smithereens in his undersea lair. Fantastic production, great performances ... but not enough laughs to persuade me to commission another full series.

There was positive press coverage too. The broadsheets picked up on John Purser's twenty-part documentary series telling the history of *Scotland's Music*, and our refurbishment of the annual *BBC Radio Scotland Young Traditional Musician* competition gave it a higher profile, as we broadcast the final live and took care to ensure that our station branding was always connected with the event and the winner.

Maggie Cunningham had launched this competition in association with the *Hands Up for Trad* body led by Simon Thoumire. Maggie had been quizzed by a committee of the Scottish Parliament about the station's support for traditional music, but she was always more enthusiastic about the genre than I ever was. Ironically, after the new-look Young Trad Final, it was said that Radio Scotland finally had a Head who appreciated traditional music. I didn't tell Maggie.

There was a period when every commercial radio station seemed to be trying stunts in the hope of getting free publicity. There was even an awards category at the Sonys for the best of these. I'd hear about listeners being married on air, or trying to set a world record for the number of people squeezing into a VW Beetle. Some stunts went horribly wrong, such as the time listeners at a radio event were challenged to see who could sit for the longest time on a block of ice. There was a mix-up, and this turned out to be a block of dry ice – frozen CO_2 – instead of water, and a number of people were hospitalised.

I wasn't averse to doing the odd thing to get us noticed but felt better if the idea had some integrity. In 2007, producer Muslim Alim persuaded me to participate in 'No Music Day'. This had stemmed from former KLF frontman, Bill Drummond, who had been arguing that there was now so much music available that it was being cheapened as an art form, and people were taking it for granted. Muslim set about organising the removal of all music from the Radio Scotland schedule, including from news and travel stings, programme trails and, of course, our evening music shows, where the presenters and producers came up with innovative ideas to have music-related content – guests and interviews – without playing any records. In its own way, it also highlighted how much Radio Scotland actually supported live music across genres, ranging from rock and pop, to folk and classical. In our publicity for No Music Day I was able to state that Radio Scotland played more live music than all of Scotland's commercial stations put together. This was before stations like Clyde and Forth relaunched their showcase for indie bands, so it wasn't a hard claim to make.

Another musical artist that brought us to the attention of the press was Amy Winehouse. When the Radio Festival was staged at Glasgow's City Halls in 2008, I was asked to take part in a panel discussion about radio journalism, entitled 'Winehouse or Whitehouse'. Chaired by Vanessa Feltz, panellists had to attach or defend the notion that entertainment wasn't real news. The session producer had been having trouble getting anyone to argue against the entertainment side, so I stepped in and spent a disquieting few hours preparing my spiel by looking at coverage of artists like Pete Doherty and Amy Winehouse. Knowing how some of these panel sessions could look on paper and then dissolve into dullness, I decided I wouldn't pull my punches. I suggested that Radio 1 had curtailed their coverage of Doherty's drug-induced antics because 'he wasn't dying fast enough', and that if we continued to air stories about Amy Winehouse's downward spiral then we would be complicit in her destruction. I argued that if we were really concerned about young people destroying themselves through drink and drugs, then we needed only to look a mile down the road from the festival venue and see what was happening to young people in the East End of Glasgow. That statement received a round of applause, but my forthright views were not to everyone's liking, especially when newspaper coverage gave the impression that I had been attacking the BBC's role in celebrity crash and burn stories. Three years later, of course, Amy Winehouse died of alcohol poisoning. She was twenty-seven years old.

Overt attempts to garner headlines tend to backfire because newspaper reporters don't like being manipulated. And, I'll say it again, the ideas that seem great when you're having a laugh and a few drinks with pals should immediately be binned the following morning – not so my decision to 'ban' a Christmas single that had been produced by Richard Melvin called 'Santa's a Scotsman' – famous for its funniest lyrics: 'Too many pies, not enough exercise, of course he's one of us'.

In my daily blog, I had been writing about the BBC's history of banning certain records, and how that usually ended with the track hitting the top of the charts. The only sure route to success for a Christmas single, I explained, was to have it banned by a radio station. As an experiment therefore, I was going to ban 'Santa's a Scotsman' on the spurious grounds that it stereotyped Scottish people as overweight gluttons. Of course, Richard was the co-conspirator in this and, when contacted by *The Edinburgh Evening News* for comment, he expressed his shock and disappointment at the decision. He then went a little further than I had expecting by accusing me of trying to gather publicity on the back of his success. Friends like that, eh?

Back on my blog I rescinded my ban and offered the following po-faced climb-down statement to the press:

> I now accept that the song does have artistic
> merit and, moreover, it is probably the case that
> Santa is indeed a Scot. I accept that lyrics
> which refer to Scots as pie-munchers with a
> weight problem were intended as a bit of fun.
> As someone who last experienced fun in 1978,
> I have difficulty recognising it in others.

'Santa's a Scotsman' did indeed get to No. 1 (albeit on a Scottish digital download chart) and, every festive season, is a favourite of Ken Bruce on BBC Radio 2. Richard Melvin thanked me with the delivery of 500 Brussels sprouts to my office.

Vegetable payola. Don't tell the newspapers.

15.

A BIT TACKY, BUT IT STICKS

If you find yourself leafing through an old copy of *The Big Issue* magazine, specifically the Scottish edition from 30th April, 1998, you will find on page 32 a half-page article about Ford Kiernan and Greg Hemphill. They are described as the presenters of a Radio Scotland series entitled *Chewin' the Fat* and Ford is quoted thus: 'We just shoot the breeze and have a laugh, but we also have some regular characters like the Hillbillies and the tit-fixated surgeon'.

The main focus of the article is not on the radio series, however, but on the writing partners' new play about two grumpy old men living in a tower-block flat in Glasgow. The production of *Still Game* had been packing them in at the Arches Theatre and was now heading for a run in Belfast. As Scottish comedy fans will testify, *Chewin' the Fat* moved from radio to television and became a hit sketch show. *Still Game* was developed as a television sitcom and took on almost legendary status. So, we all know what happened to Ford and Greg ... but what became of the bespectacled comedian pictured in an article on the previous page of that week's *Big Issue*? Yes, flip back and you'll find a review of some open-mic auditions that had taken place in the foyer of the Kings Theatre in Glasgow. These were being held by the Comedy Store; their first such foray outside London. The article begins with some cruel descriptions of the first few contenders as 'dreadful' and 'chronic', but the review continues:

> Just when all seemed lost, a genuine, 24-carat side-splitting, destined for international fame, undiscovered comic genius takes to the stage. Johnny Sellotape, inventor of 'adhesive humour' – a bit tacky but it sticks – and owner of the most ridiculous catchphrase in comedy – 'Uhu the Noo!' – shatters the tangible tension that's been building up so far. 'I used to have a partner, Billy Blu Tac,' he announces deadpan. 'We dared to defy the conventions of a double-act in that we were both straight men.'
>
> "Billy, how fat's your mother-in-law?" I'd ask.
>
> "Not very," Billy would say. "She's been on a diet."' The room erupts.

Johnny Sellotape and Craig Hill were two of the chosen finalists that night and a few weeks later Johnny appeared on the main stage at the King's in the company of seasoned professionals like Paul Zenon and Rhona Cameron. The newcomers' performances were judged by an audience clapometer device and the enthusiastic applause for Craig Hill kick-started his career. Alas, the clapometer was not kind to Johnny Sellotape and not much was heard of him until Radio Scotland ran a spoof documentary – *Stuck*! – about his life and times. He made one guest appearance as the on-air producer of Austin Lafferty's late-night phone-in show, *Lafferty Out Loud*, but *The Big Issue's* forecast of international fame did not come to pass and I can tell you why that was. You see, I was Johnny Sellotape.

My appearance at those auditions and the subsequent final was the result of a stupid dare that just went a little bit too far. I was standing in one of our production offices when I heard mention of the Comedy Store's forthcoming show in Glasgow and, somewhat cynically, I suggested that the open auditions might just be a publicity stunt. Goaded into taking part, I looked around the office for some inspiration, but all I could see were office supplies, and so Johnny Sellotape was born. And his daft gimmick of attaching old jokes to his jacket would allow him to fill the required five minutes of stage time, should he forget his lines.

It had, all the same, given me first-hand experience of stand-up comedy and by that, I don't just mean the gut-wrenching feeling as you walk on stage, nor the mild panic when the audience doesn't laugh. I'm also talking about what happens backstage: the worry, the paranoia and the feeling of sheer loneliness as you await your few minutes in the limelight.

I could begin to imagine the life of a touring comedian, travelling from town to town, walking off stage with that burst of adrenaline just as everyone else was looking forward to going home to bed. No wonder so many comedians ended up in late-night bars and clubs, frittering away whatever cash they had earned, buying drinks or anything else that was offered.

I love comedy and I love radio comedy in particular. When school pals were building their record collections with the latest chart-toppers, I was rifling through second-hand shops looking for albums of *The Goons*, *The Glums*, *Round the Horne* and other audio delights, such as the recordings of American comedians like Bob Newhart, Woody Allen and Shelley Berman. When I got the job running Radio Scotland – seven years after Johnny Sellotape's debut – I was keen to open the airwaves to some new talent. That also meant saying goodbye to some long-running audience favourites like *Watson's Wind-Up*, and shelving another series of Sanjeev Kohli's *Lunchtime Tonight*. This prompted Sanjeev to tell *The Sunday Times* that Radio Scotland comedy was 'woeful,' 'pedestrian' and 'monochromatic' – so no hard feelings there!

I had commissioned *The Franz Kafka Big Band* because I knew the writers and performers had a feeling for playing with words and sounds. The other sketch comedy from Demus Productions, *Sabotage*, offered yet more new talent on air. In-house producer Margaret-Anne Docherty had created the female-focused show *The Y-Front*, with Elaine MacKenzie Ellis and Julie Coombe, and later paired Elaine with a young Des Clarke for a series called *Ellis Island*. She also produced several series of a sitcom called *Free-Falling* and worked with the Aberdeen-based stage comedy team,

Flying Pig, to bring the hugely popular series *Desperate Fishwives* to radio and then to a TV pilot.

There were misses as well as hits, as I offered comedy pilots to a whole range of companies and producers who tried fresh ideas with new writers and performers. My own tastes in comedy are fairly eclectic, so I admired a gentle series such as *Piano Lessons*, in which Bill Paterson played a life-ravaged music teacher, just as I loved the broader laughs that came from the original radio version of *Burnistoun*. *The Bob Servant Emails* was adapted from Neil Forsyth's books about the pompous Dundonian. The actor Brian Cox played Bob on radio and also, following the success of the series, in the television version. I was also keen to reflect the wealth of talent on the Scottish stand-up circuit and we recorded a special cabaret comedy night on the Renfrew Ferry – a floating restaurant on the Clyde – with a line-up that included Raymond Mearns, Susan Calman, Greg McHugh and Miles Jupp.

The Edinburgh Fringe was, of course, the place to spot new talent and the trending themes. One year, in particular, it seemed that every stand-up was exploring their own psychology and discussing tough issues such as their own mental health. One that stood out for me was Juliette Burton's show, *When I Grow Up*. It began as a light-hearted piece about how Juliette, now a grown woman, tried to realise the dreams that she had as a little girl. These included having a hit single, marrying a prince and becoming a Muppet. Juliette's show took an unexpected turn when she revealed to the audience the reason she had not been able to pursue those dreams: her teenage years had been blighted by eating disorders which had almost killed her, and at one stage had led to her being sectioned under the Mental Health Act. Other comedians on the Fringe that year were exploring similar issues and, chatting this through with Julia Sutherland and Richard Melvin, we decided to showcase a half-dozen such performers in a series for Radio Scotland. Julia had been compering comedy nights at the Vespbar venue in Glasgow and had begun to build a reputation for presenting radio shows that combined stand-up comedy with tough interviews around topics such as mental health, bereavement and racism. Her long-running series *The Funny Life of ...* allowed comedians to describe the real-life experiences that had been the source material for their jokes. The best example of this was the edition featuring the young comedian Ashley Storrie, whose childhood experiences had been tainted by Glasgow's gangland culture.

All of this reminded me of a comedy workshop I'd attended as part of Dan O'Day's radio seminar in Hollywood. He had invited Ken Levine – a writer with *M.A.S.H.* and *Cheers* – to talk to us about his career and give us one simple exercise. Assuring us that no one would be asked to read anything aloud, he invited us to spend ten minutes writing about something that was worrying us or had troubled us in our past; even a childhood memory would suffice. We followed his instructions and, safe in the knowledge that no one would see what I had written, I scribbled out a few lines about being bullied at primary school. Bullying was such a common occurrence in my schooldays that it might as well have been part of the curriculum. In my case, it was a short-lived episode where a new boy in class had preyed upon those of us who were flush with lunch money, or had disposable cash for the tuck shop. It had been a long time ago, but I still felt uneasy thinking about it.

Ken Levine then told us to take a break, look at what we had written and then re-write it, looking for the funny side. This time, he said, we would be asked to tell everyone what we had come up with. I turned my bullying story into an exaggerated tale about a playground protection racket and how I had recruited bodyguards from the ranks of fellow pupils, paying them from my hoard of chocolate bars and toffee chews. Others on the workshop came up with similar tales and when you heard about funny incidents at a funeral or hilarious goings-on in a cancer ward, you could only guess at the real-life horror that had been mined for laughs. The ability to turn grim but recognisable reality into comedy was what lay behind the success of so many of the guests on Julia's shows, but it did make you wonder where the bodies were buried.

Alongside stand-up and sit-coms, I was always keen to find a winning format for a panel show, and back in my days in charge of topical programmes, I had come up with the idea of guests trying to predict the following week's news. We piloted it as a one-off for the Christmas schedule and called it *Next Year's News*. Gary Robertson invited a comedian, an astrologer and a weather forecaster to match their predictions against those made in an opinion poll. It didn't quite come off and, some years later, Channel 4 had more success with *8 Out of 10 Cats*, which included comedians and opinion polls, but without the forecasting nonsense.

Those panel formats are difficult to get right, but I think we struck gold when Des Clarke agreed to host *Breaking the News,* a quiz in which 'Radio Scotland breaks the news and invites four opinionated panellists to put it back together again'. Not only did the show offer a way of laughing at divisive issues such as Scottish politics and football, it also offered a platform for a new generation of comedians who were forging their careers on the club circuit. Also, because we insisted that no show could be produced with an imbalance of male guests, it gave the lie to the notion that there were no talented female comedians on the scene. Alongside Julia and Ashley there were Jay Lafferty, Janey Godley, Fern Brady, Keara Murphy, Susie McCabe, Susan Calman, Jo Caulfield, and many more.

Comedy and comedians continue to fascinate me and I think, as an art form, stand-up comedy is massively underrated. If you stage a drama and the applause isn't enthusiastic you can pretend the audience didn't understand the deeper meaning or were perhaps too busy thinking to clap. You can write a humorous column in a newspaper and hope people smile as they read it. But if you stand in a basement comedy club for twenty minutes and hit paying customers with your best stuff, there's no hiding place if no one laughs. You might imagine that my short-lived career as Johnny Sellotape would have scarred me for life, but a few years ago, Julia Sutherland challenged me to do five minutes during a 'new material' night at Vespbar, now renamed 'Yesbar'. This was not the same as a 'new talent' night, because it involved professionals trying out new jokes and routines before they decided to bin them or take them on the road. So, I found myself on the same bill as Gary Little – a fifty-something former jailbird who had the crowd in stiches with his routine about walking a talking dog in a Glasgow park. I stepped up to the microphone, not as Johnny Sellotape, but as Jeff – a man on the wrong side of fifty, whose children were about to leave home for university and who was attempting to fill the gaps in his life. As Ken Levine had taught us that afternoon in Hollywood, the best material comes from the things that you are most worried about. I got some laughs. Maybe they were more *about* me than *with* me, but I took what I could get.

My try-anything philosophy also had me agreeing to take part in a Goons-style stage show that had been running for several weeks in a basement bar in Edinburgh. This was written by Lach, the same American performer that Richard Melvin had befriended in New York and who had subsequently decided to move permanently to Scotland. Unbeknown to me, a recurring but unseen character in these weekly shows was the Head of Radio Scotland. When Lach wrote an episode in which this radio boss was kidnapped by a mad Highland crofter he called me and asked if I would be willing to play the part myself and bring this unseen character to life. A few nights later I found myself on stage, as crazy Mistress MacKenzie, played by Keara Murphy, wrapped me in duct tape. It was a bit of a laugh, but the director's notes afterwards were crushing.

Apparently, my performance as the Head of Radio Scotland was ... *unconvincing*.

16.

OLD FIRM DAY

Were it not for my wife and son, Radio Scotland might have abandoned its coverage of Scottish football and replaced it with full-length performances of opera. That threat was one I seriously suggested to our Sport Editor, Tom Connor, when he updated me about the latest wranglings with football clubs, their managers or, more often, their Board of Directors.

BBC Sport, like BBC News, is a separate directorate, but at least the radio sports department in Glasgow would invite me to their meetings, although I doubt if they ever found my input useful. When, for example, they asked for my thoughts on the commentary of a game in Inverness, I heaped praise on the presenter's vivid and poetic description of the sun setting over the Moray Firth as glimpsed from the commentary position. This had happened during the half-time interval. Asked about the match itself – a nil-nil draw – I opined that it might have been useful to have made the game sound a little less dull than it obviously had been because, well ... making programmes that were worth listening to was kinda the point.

Hearing pundits use phrases like 'absolutely nothing happening here at all' was bad enough, but it was worse when they complained about having to travel all the way up the A9 to cover the game, forgetting that fans in the north often had to make a similar journey south for the away ties. Having said that, when there was a big game, with a lot at stake, there was nothing to match the skills and knowledge of presenters like Richard Gordon and commentators like Liam McLeod. You didn't have to be a football fan to appreciate their ability to describe 'every kick of the ball' and keep you hanging on every word as you waited for the final result.

There always seemed to be one club or another threatening to ban us from their ground or their press conferences because they had taken exception to something said by one of our reporters. This was despite the fact that BBC Sport spent millions of pounds of licence-payers' money to secure the broadcast rights, and despite clubs having signed contracts that supposedly guaranteed post-match interviews with managers or players. I compared these dummy-out-of-the-pram antics with the professionalism with which these conditions were honoured at, say, Wimbledon or during the Olympics. What made matters worse was that, in the period when BBC Scotland had exclusive rights to top-flight Scottish football, Radio Clyde managed to mount respectable editions of their *Superscoreboard* programme by offering goal flashes and match updates just moments after they had been broadcast by the BBC.

By looping a soundtrack of match atmosphere behind their presenters and reporters, they gave the impression they were still at the heart of the action. It was pretty clever stuff and cost them very little. Frustrating as it was, my argument wasn't with Radio Clyde, it was with the football authorities who didn't seem to police and protect their rights, inevitably reducing the value of them when it came to the next round of contract negotiations.

'Tell them to stuff it,' I used to tell Tom. 'We'll leave men's football to commercial radio and champion the women's game instead. We could spend that money on comedy or drama or ... or ... opera, or whatever.'

As Tom peeled me off the ceiling, he would remind me that tens of thousands of licence-paying listeners actually loved our coverage of Scottish football and I knew he was right. Among them were Anne and Alan, who had become diehard fans of Inverness Caledonian Thistle and, on Saturdays, would listen to Radio Scotland from the start of *Off the Ball* and only switch off as they heard Robbie Shepherd's signature tune for *Take the Floor*. Alan had hero-worshipped Terry Butcher, the former England captain, who had taken charge of 'Caley Thistle' just as they slumped into the relegation zone and had then secured their promotion the following year. That hero-worship lasted until the very day that Butcher took a new job at Hibs, at which point he became a forgotten man.

Boardroom and dugout dramas were as much a part of Radio Scotland's coverage as the games themselves and even football agnostics like me enjoyed the stories that went with it.

Back when I was still Editor for Topical and Events, an idea had come to me as I was driving past Ibrox stadium.

I thought about all the different people and organisations who became involved whenever there was a match between Celtic and Rangers, the so-called 'Old Firm'. There were the players themselves, of course, and the fans, but also the referee, the press reporters, the souvenir-sellers, the bus and train drivers and, sadly, the ambulance crews and the police. I wondered how we might tell the story of an Old Firm Day in Scotland and that's when I remembered Capital Radio's *Day in the Life of London*, and how it had offered me one of my first opportunities as a student journalist. We could do the same kind of thing around a match between Celtic and Rangers.

We put the word out to universities and colleges around Scotland and recruited around twenty media and journalism students. Each was paired with a member of BBC Scotland staff who would act as their mentor up to and beyond the day itself. We brought the students in for a day of training and briefing, and then assigned them, mostly in pairs for safety, to cover different aspects of the match day. One pair would follow a Celtic fan from dawn to dusk, and another would do likewise with a Rangers supporter. Another student tagged along with the referee, another was in the BBC TV outside broadcast van, yet another shadowed a *Daily Record* sports reporter, and so on. It would be up to producer Stephen Hollywood to pull the whole thing together, and his final documentary, *Old Firm Day*, went on to win a Sony award. It offered a real glimpse of one aspect of Glasgow's culture and how supporters' rivalry could range from good-humoured exchanges of insults to real, deep-seated hatred and bigotry which, when fuelled by alcohol, could end in violence and tragedy. The project also gave a foot in the door to students like Annie McGuire and Martin Dowden who, a few years later, joined BBC Scotland's Sport team.

My comment to Tom about women's football was not the throwaway remark it might have sounded. At about the same time we were making *Old Firm Day*, I heard a report about Julie Fleeting, a top striker with Scotland's national women's team, who had been offered the chance to play for a professional team in San Diego. I thought this also had the makings of an interesting documentary and travelled down to her home in Kilwinning to interview Julie alongside her parents, as they discussed her big move to America. The women's game appeared to be taking off in the States and San Diego Spirit was one of eight teams in a brand-new league. After recording the interviews in her parents' kitchen, I decided, unwisely, to grab some actuality of Julie as she jogged around a local playing field. Trying to keep up with her would have been hard at the best of times but doing so in my office suit while carrying a tape machine and brandishing a microphone almost ended me. Asthmatic wheezing on my part rendered most of that recording unusable.

As Julie arrived in San Diego, I had arranged for freelance reporter Maggie Shiels to pick up the story at that end and we got a real flavour of how much effort went into promoting the game and making it a family-friendly event for fans. There was much talk about the 'match-day experience', and music and razzmatazz was laid on for parents and kids who had been persuaded to watch a game of soccer instead of visiting a shopping mall or sunning themselves at the beach. I thought of this often as I shivered alongside Anne and Alan at Caley Stadium, where the match-day experience involved a lukewarm pie and a plastic cup of Bovril, and the razzmatazz amounted to some poor soul in a loose-fitting Nessie costume trying to keep his trousers hoisted as he wandered along the touchline as the team mascot.

I imagined how the documentary on Julie Fleeting might end: she either would or would not be offered a permanent place on the team, and either would or would not accept it; she would either be staying there or coming home. But as the weeks went on, Julie seemed to have trouble making up her mind and we had to transmit the programme inconclusively, before she made a final decision, before she was named the team's most valuable player and, alas, before the league itself collapsed after just three seasons. Still, it had offered Radio Scotland listeners a different version of football and was an early sign of how the women's game would take off in Scotland in future years.

One final word on opera, though. Not long after I was appointed as Head of Radio, I made contact with an old friend from Easterhouse. Paul Curran and I had both been members of the school orchestra. He had played the clarinet like a maestro and I had played the baritone horn like an apprentice plumber testing the brass pipework for leaks. In the intervening years he had built a career, first in ballet and then as a respected and much sought-after opera director. He had, for a time, been General Manager of the Norwegian National Opera, and had gone on to direct performances at the Met in New York, as well as in places as far-flung as Moscow and Los Angeles. On a flying visit to Glasgow, we met up for a drink at the Radisson Hotel and easily fell back into relaxed conversation about our schooldays and our different career paths. Towards the end of that chat he asked if the Radio Scotland schedule included much opera and, with some guilt, I had to admit it didn't.

If only Tom Connor had listened to me.

17.

FORTRESS RADIO

When I got the job as Head of Radio I was overly fond of annoying and confusing people by telling them that I was not, in fact, the Head of Radio Scotland.

'It's about that comma between Radio and Scotland,' I would explain, qualifying as I did so for the Pedant of the Year competition. As Head of Radio, Scotland, or Head of Radio at BBC Scotland, I also had responsibility for the production teams who developed and pitched programme offers to the BBC's UK radio networks, such as Radio 1 and Radio 4. By and large, that process happened without my involvement because the Network Controllers or Commissioning Editors had forged good and long-standing relationships with their favourite producers in Glasgow and Edinburgh, and trusted them to deliver high-quality content with an understanding of the target audience.

A producer like Mark Rickards, for example, worked almost exclusively for Radio 4 and BBC World Service. He was occasionally glimpsed in his supposed base of Edinburgh, but more often than not he would be roaming the world, making a fascinating documentary in the Amazonian rainforest, or maybe unearthing signs of an ancient tribe in Central Africa. Similarly, his colleague David Stenhouse was more than just a fountain of ideas. I thought of David as an 'Oxbridge whisperer' because he spoke the same language as the Radio 4 Commissioning Editors who had been educated at Oxford and Cambridge. Unsophisticated journalists like me could recognise a good story well told, but I was bewildered when commissioners asked for programmes with a 'delicious texture'. Were we talking about radio or baking?

Pitching to Radio 4 took more patience than I could ever muster. Jane Fowler tells the story of offering an idea about the emerging music scene in Glasgow and having to give constant assurances that the final programme would not include bagpipe music because, she was informed, that would not sit well with the station's heartland, Middle-England audience. Jane had no intention of including bagpipes and gave lengthy explanations about the new generation of music-makers, many of them producing tracks in back bedrooms and high-rise flats. Bagpipes would not feature at all, she insisted. No chance. Then, as the long conversation drew to a close, the Commissioning Editor suddenly suggested that there should be at least some passing reference to the legacy of bagpipe music. In fact, she insisted upon it. To which Jane simply said, 'Of course.'

Network Radio had a much bigger budget than Radio Scotland but, with a frozen licence fee and a set of new priorities in the digital world, the BBC demanded savings and efficiencies from all quarters. Years of resistance to making cuts had earned this division of the Corporation the nickname 'Fortress Radio', but the time had come when even Radio 4 had to start counting the pennies.

This, in turn, led to a continuing decline in the amount of programming being bought from the Nations and in Scotland; we started to feel the chill. Although it could be imagined that supplying programmes to those comparatively well-funded services might have allowed us to break even or even earn a small profit, the opposite turned out to be the case. It was particularly true when it came to making one-off documentaries or even a short series of speech programmes. The trouble was that there was not enough volume to give economies of scale. As part of my NASA-style exploration of our accounts, I had discovered that funds meant for Radio Scotland were being diverted to subsidise the true cost of making programmes for the UK networks. The figures were not small: over the years it added up to millions of pounds.

When my feet were more firmly under the table, I made efforts to build relationships with my opposite numbers in London and around the other BBC Nations. When the annual Radio Festival was staged in Edinburgh, I saw this as a good opportunity for hobnobbing with radio's power elite. My first approach was to the Controller of Radio 2, Lesley Douglas, who I spotted in the foyer of the Festival venue, the Edinburgh International Conference Centre. As I walked towards her, I was pleasantly surprised to see her smile widen. I had met her only a few times in the preceding years but doubted she would have remembered me. It seemed I was wrong, although she did seem confused when I shook her hand and launched into some small talk about the conference sessions. It turned out she thought I was the driver come to take her to the airport. Had I only thought to wear my peaked hat that day, I could have made myself a few bob on the side.

The woman who was then in ultimate control of the Fortress was the Director of Radio, Jenny Abramsky. She threw out words like ninja stars and twice I saw her chair a meeting with her shoeless feet on the table in front of us as she fired off questions to the various participants and, with shrewd use of body language, simply ignored the people whose opinions she did not rate. I was present at a meeting of her Radio Controllers for a grim presentation on the performance of BBC Radio in Scotland's major cities. Given the popularity of commercial radio, Radio 2 and Radio Scotland in Glasgow, it was no surprise that other BBC stations were not doing especially well in that city. This revelation, however, seemed to shock Jenny Abramsky, who described it bluntly as 'failure'. Having no direct line-management connection with the Director of Radio, I was able to watch gleefully as the experienced and intelligent Controllers of Radios 1 to 5 averted their gaze as if suddenly finding something fascinating about the coffee cups in front of them or the fruit on the sideboard. No one wanted to catch her eye or incur her wrath. Finally, it was Mark Damazer, Controller of Radio 4 and a man known as 'Two-Brains Damazer', who was brave enough to break the silence.

'I knew I should have taken today off as a duvet day.'

Our radio editors in Scotland – Bruce Young for Drama, Helen Munro for Music, and Jane Fowler for Arts and Features – were heartened by the positive feedback they and their teams were getting from the network's Heads. Drama was seen as a particular strength in Scotland, as Bruce and his team recreated epic sea battles for the *Master and Commander* plays, secured actor Brian Cox for series after series of *McLevy*, and scared the pants out of Middle England with a production of *The Exorcist*.

When it came to cutbacks, however, it seemed that out of sight was out of mind. The weekly opt-out shows, which Scotland, Wales and Northern Ireland made for Radio 1, were among the first casualties. I may be wrong, but I put this down to ill-advised honesty from the Editor of Radio Ulster, who admitted that we were all making a tidy sum from that commission and were using the surplus to offset the losses we made on other network programmes. This might have been true, but I can't imagine the Controller of Radio 1 was particularly pleased to discover he was atoning for the tight-fistedness of his sister stations.

Each commissioning round brought with it rollercoasters of hope and disappointment when shortlisted offers failed to make it to the final commissioning list. Radio 2, for example, would often list thirty or more of our offers and then, by decision day, opt for just one or two half-hour documentaries. The budget for these was barely enough to justify the costs of the flights to London for the original pitching session. I caught such a flight to head south and discuss the situation with Lesley Douglas, combining it with a meeting of the Radio Academy Awards Committee, so I ended up having tea with Lesley in a little café off Baker Street.

'Don't let me forget to pay for these,' she told me, as the waitress set down our cups. 'I'm forever doing that in cafés and restaurants because I forget that I'm not in the BBC canteen.'

Notwithstanding the fact that the BBC canteen was not a free-for-all, this curious admission made me wonder if people who spent too much time ensconced in Broadcasting House began to lose touch with reality. I was tempted to ask her if she knew the price of a pint of milk, but since I didn't know myself, I let it go. Lesley promised to address the offers and shortlist problems, but very little changed and she herself fell victim to the infamous Ross–Brand scandal after giving a one-word answer – 'yes' – when a worried producer called to ask if a pre-recorded sequence of Russel Brand making sex jokes with Jonathon Ross should actually be transmitted. The ensuing row had forced the Director General to cut short a holiday in America and fly back to deal with it. That's never a good thing.

Bob Shennan, who then took over at Radio 2, was a much easier figure to deal with. At the very least, he seemed like the kind of man who always paid for his own tea without prompting. Bob had been away from the BBC for a period after being head-hunted to run a digital radio service for Channel 4 Television, but when that came to nothing, he came back to the Beeb and was widely welcomed. On Radio Scotland, Ricky Ross, frontman with the band Deacon Blue, had won numerous awards and the respect of musicians for his show *Another Country*, and Bob was keen to hear more of Ricky on Radio 2. That, together with

Helen Munro's leadership of a pan-BBC approach to jazz, opened up new opportunities for music producers in Glasgow. On the downside, however, Radio 4 was making slow but painful cuts to drama and readings, and eventually started landing heavy blows such as the decommissioning of the *Four O'clock Show* on the digital station Radio 4 Extra.

In my time as Head of Radio in Scotland, I must have written a dozen different strategy papers about our relationship with the BBC networks. I could point to the win-win situation that had arisen when Mary Kalemkerian was running the digital station BBC 7 and wanted more new comedy for her schedule. At that time, Dabster Productions had offered me a simple effective format, featuring Sarah Millican introducing and interviewing fellow comedians at The Stand Comedy Club in Edinburgh. Pooling my limited commissioning cash with Mary's, I was able to up the number of episodes I could afford from eight to twelve. I ran *Sarah at the Stand* first on Radio Scotland, then BBC 7, being a digital station with a different rights arrangement, could run each episode ten times. Meanwhile Dabster got a twelve-part commission instead of eight. Everyone was happy. When Mary retired and BBC 7 became Radio 4 Extra, the new commissioner bought just six episodes of the follow-up series and bought them directly from Dabster. Out of the loop, I contributed nothing and couldn't run them in Scotland, and Dabster got paid for six episodes instead of twelve.

This kind of silliness had me banging my head against a wall, because it wasn't all about money and business; it was about the success of the BBC in Scotland. Year after year we could see that these networks, with the exception of Radio 2, were performing well below average in Scotland. It wasn't just that the money was concentrated in London, but that the commissioning decisions were being made from that metropolitan point of view. It meant that the version of Scotland that the audience heard on network radio was the version that was understood by a small number of London commissioners – they had heard of Sir Walter Scott and Billy Connolly, but it was trickier persuading them to take a risk on new Scottish writers or new Scottish comedians.

More relevant programming from Scotland might have helped, but there was no will to address it and that was understandable up to a point. At a UK level, stations like Radio 4 and Radio 2 were hitting some of their highest audience figures of all time. What did it matter if only 2 per cent of those programmes came from Scotland? True, BBC Television had been given an instruction to commission around 9 per cent of its programmes from Scotland and that was measured and enforced. In a speech at Pacific Quay, Mark Thompson had said that radio should be included in that percentage too, but he may have said it without realising the implications and, in any case, it was never followed up.

Fortress Radio remained intact.

18.

HALL OF FAME

I was lunching at the Savoy Hotel in London. I've always wanted to write a sentence like that. It makes me feel like I'm about to tell some spiffing tale in the style of John Buchan or Ian Fleming and attempt to enthral you with some yarn involving a rich business tycoon or members of the Royal Family. And, you know, I'm about to do exactly that, but first I have to tell you about that lunch at the Savoy and a tale that does involve a hero and a villain.

The occasion was the annual Induction Ceremony into the Radio Academy Hall of Fame. It was, then, one of the Academy's three set-piece events, alongside the Sony Awards and the Radio Festival. The lunch was a small-scale invitation-only affair, usually attended by the top execs in the BBC and their counterparts from commercial radio and other industry bodies. This year, however, I was surprised to get an invitation to sit at the Nations and Regions table, alongside some colleagues from Wales and Northern Ireland. I like to assume that my invitation was just one of the perks of my new job, and not because others had suddenly discovered conflicting appointments when they heard that one guest of honour would be Jimmy Savile. His name was wiped from the Academy's Roll of Honour when his crimes came to light, so my account of his nonsensical babbling that particular afternoon can also be popped in the bin.

Among the various radio stars dotted around the room, I had spotted one of my all-time heroes. It wasn't a rock star or a famous DJ, but the former editor of *Punch* magazine, Alan Coren. He was now a regular on Radio 4's *News Quiz* and was among others who had come to pay tribute to fellow panellist the late Linda Smith. I had been an avid reader of *Punch* in my late teens, and it is still a proud boast that I won its famous cartoon caption competition no less than three – count them! – *three* times. I bought the magazine for two reasons. The first was for the writing of Alan Coren, who could choose any subject, even a single line from a newspaper story, and, in a few hundred words, take us on a hilarious flight of fancy. A story suggesting that James Bond was getting too old, for example, included the memorable line 'Bond tensed and reached for his teeth'. The second reason was the *Father's Day* column penned by Hunter Davies. Here the laughs came from his authentic observations of family life and, many years before Sarah and Alan came along, I had gained at least an inkling of what modern parenthood might be like. Of course, he mainly told us the fun stuff.

So, there was Alan Coren at the next table, and there was I, in two minds about approaching him because the occasion didn't seem right. He was there to honour the memory of a much-loved friend. It would be crass, would it not, to sidle up to that table and blurt out memories of his days at *Punch*? But maybe, if he was on his own at some point …

As I was mulling this over, I hadn't spotted that the ceremony had finished and people were starting to leave. The adjacent table was now being cleared and there was no sign of Alan Coren. I slurped my coffee, pocketed my after-dinner mint and made my way down to the hotel's famous American Bar. I ordered a whisky and kept a watchful eye out for my hero, but he was gone. When, the following year, I heard of Alan Coren's death, I regretted my hesitancy that afternoon and wished I had gone over to say a simple hello. Thinking of this recently I wrote, via his publisher, to Hunter Davies and told him as best I could about how I had enjoyed *his* columns and books. They relayed back his thanks and appreciation.

To be honest, I'm not much good with famous people unless I have a microphone in my hand and a reason to interview them. It's not that I get star-struck: my father taught me that you should treat everyone with exactly the amount of respect and contempt that they deserved. Mike Ungersma, our American lecturer at Cardiff, put it in his own way: 'Don't get blinded by the stars, kids,' he would tell us. 'Just remember that these guys pull up their pants one leg at a time just like the rest of us.'

The thing is, I'm never quite sure how these famous folk want to be treated. Do they like a bit of fawning and, as Jay Leno told me, regard each handshake as another new viewer or listener? Or do they perceive every stranger who approaches them as a potential threat, a would-be stalker or an annoying requester of selfies? If only every famous encounter came with easy-to-follow instructions, like you get from the Royal Family.

Take that time I met Princess Anne, the Princess Royal. Her Royal Highness was the very, very special guest of honour at the opening of a Sense Centre for blind and deaf children in Glasgow. This had been partially funded by donations to Children in Need, so a handful of BBC bods were invited to listen to the speeches and then head upstairs afterwards to join the Princess and other dignitaries for a spot of hospitality, and a bit of a chinwag.

Among the people in the room was a woman who told me she was the Duchess of Sutherland. This reminded me of the statue of the Duke of Sutherland that had featured in one episode of *Blokes on Blocks*, but tact prevented me from mentioning that or asking if she was directly related to the man who had cleared the Highlands of crofters and replaced them with sheep – a rare moment of common sense from me.

As we all waited for the Princess, we got instructions on the strict protocol that must be adhered to when the royal presence was among us. We were formed into groups of five and told to stand in a little semicircle. The person first greeted by the Princess should introduce the rest of the group and – this was very important! – none of us should speak to her unless she had already spoken to us. The Princess arrived and, because our group was nearest to the door, she approached us first. That's when things started to go wrong. The lead figure in our semicircle shook the royal glove but neglected to introduce the rest of us. As a result, she looked at each of us in turn with a bemused and quizzical expression, probably wondering who the heck we were. We, of course, were waiting for her to speak to us and stuck diligently to our promised vow of silence. This started to feel like a bit of a stand-off. Who was going to blab first? She did. The Princess asked one of those innocuous questions about the location of this new Sense Centre and whether it would be convenient for the children and families who hoped to use it. This, to our relief, prompted an explosion of conversation about the transport links in this part of Glasgow – Govan – and a small debate about which bus routes best served the area. BBC Scotland's Children in Need champion, the amiable Fraser Falconer, went a bit further than he needed to by specifying the precise routes and numbers of each service, sometimes contradicting himself and back-tracking.

'I think the number 34 is your best bet,' he told her. 'No, hold that thought, no you're much better getting on the 34A, because that will take you straight past the door. On Sundays though, you're better off catching the 304.'

I could see the Princess absorb this information with a concentrated frown, but there was no sign of her taking notes for future reference. I, meanwhile, continued to stare at her. She hadn't yet spoken directly to me, so I said nothing. I tried to communicate my enjoyment of her company with smiles and nods, and I was considering staging some kind of hand shadow display when she made a little joke. There then ensued much over-the-top guffawing. I hadn't actually heard the joke, but I joined in with the laughter anyway, grateful to check if my vocal chords were still intact. Satisfied with our reaction, the Princess ambled on to the next semicircle, giving me one final curious glance. We then broke formation to debrief the encounter. I was keen to know what her joke had been about, but the person next to me hadn't heard it either, nor had the one next to him. In fact, no one seemed exactly sure what she had said, but her intonation and body language had suggested mirth and we had all taken the cue from each other. To this day, I wonder about that royal gag. Had she made some clever pun concerning the bus journey or had she simply said, 'This is terribly dull, do shut up'? I think the latter is more likely.

Then there was that worried bloke I spotted one morning when I was waiting in the queue at the tea bar. Now he *really* was well known, but as my caffeine-starved brain took the precious seconds to process him, all I could do was say hello and ask if he was keeping busy and having fun. Then it dawned on me that this was Gordon Brown, who was then the Prime Minister. Keeping busy? I guess he was. Having fun? It never looked like he was.

I cringe more at memories of meeting people that I didn't know were already famous and, again, context could easily mislead you. When comedy producer Gus Beattie invited me to the Universal Club in Glasgow, he told me we would be seeing some great talent trying out new material. I misunderstood and assumed we were going to see some brand-new comedy performers. As I watched the show – a young guy doing stand-up and a young woman performing character sketches – I was impressed by their self-confidence. Even when a bin lorry decided to start loading glass bottles from the alley beside the club, the young guy wasn't put off his stride but just incorporated the interruption seamlessly into his routine. After the show, Gus introduced me to the pair and I was fulsome in my praise and found myself asking the young woman if she had gained her experience at school and college, and I assured the young man, in case he doubted it, that he would go far and should keep getting stage time.

Yes, that was my first ever encounter with Kevin Bridges and Susan Calman and I'd love to justify my stupidity by telling you that this was years before they had made the big time. Alas, just a month or so later, Kevin Bridges was doing sell-out concerts and Susan Calman was on network radio. That's when it dawned on me that Kevin had appeared on Radio Scotland's *Summer Supplement* programme way back when. It had been a new *material* night, not a new *talent* night.

I'm always much more comfortable in the company of famous radio people, perhaps because I think of myself as part of the same tribe. Walking through the streets of Glasgow with someone like Suzie McGuire, the former Radio Clyde DJ, was a salutary lesson in the power of local fame. We rarely got more than a few yards before yet another fan – usually a woman – would spot her, stop her, hug her and share their own life story. Then again, sometimes I met a radio star that I admired and wished I could re-do the whole encounter from the start. During the Edinburgh Fringe, for example, the Loft bar of the Gilded Balloon, or the VIP area of the Underbelly, is where you tend to bump into performers before and after their gigs. My meeting with veteran comedian and writer Barry Cryer was going very well until I spooked him by reciting entire lines from his *Hello Cheeky* series from the 1970s. Like that sketch set on the Serpentine boating lake in Hyde Park. 'Come in number nine, your time's up! Oh, sorry ... number six, are you all right?' Ha ha! Remember that one, Barry? No? Well, how about 'The Night Bus from Leyton Orient'? No? Oh, you have to head off? That's a shame.'

While I'm owning up to these various calamities, I might as well tell you about the time I offered some sound business advice to the entrepreneur Richard Branson. It happened one night at the Ubiquitous Chip in Glasgow's West End; the kind of upmarket bar and restaurant complex frequented, as my wife would say, by 'all you media types'. It's the closest Glasgow has to the Ivy in London and so has become a mecca for any celebrities or actors who hit town. On this particular night four of us 'media types' had gone there for a drink after work and were intrigued to see that the main ground-floor restaurant had been closed off for a private function. This turned out to be a party hosted by Richard Branson, who was thanking his staff following the opening of the new Virgin Megastore in Glasgow. Well, we were at that dangerous point in the evening between the second and third bottle of wine and so slipped past the cordon to join the fun. We then decided that it would be a pity to have come all this way (one small flight of stairs) and not see Richard Branson himself, so we devised a plan to waylay him on his way back from the toilet. As one of our number kept an eye on the Gents, the rest of us positioned ourselves in a seemingly random pattern, to ensure he had no clear route back to his table. It was like a commando operation without the camouflage paint. There were lots of those special ops signals with silent fingers pointing from eyes to the target, until one of our squad dislodged a contact lens.

No sooner did he emerge than we had him snared and after telling him what a splendid soiree he had laid on, I engaged him with some thoughts about the nature of his business empire and the potential risks of overstretching the Virgin brand. At that time, he had that name on everything from cans of cola to radio stations, as well as a train line and airline. I speculated that one downfall in any part of that business could tarnish the whole brand. He agreed, and I mentally congratulated myself on my hitherto unknown business acumen and rehearsed my response should he now ask me to go run his operation in New York. There was no immediate job offer, but he did spot that we'd finished our drinks and summoned a waiter to replenish our wine. To be honest, it wasn't hard for him to have noticed that we needed more drinks because one of my colleagues was tapping on the side of his empty glass and dropping subtle hints along the lines of: 'Richard, we need more wine here.'

Our conversation now turned to the location of his new Megastore. Emboldened by his reaction to my previous words of wisdom, I now vouchsafed the view that, 'Richard, honestly, no word of a lie, that new store of yours is in entirely the wrong part of the city centre.' He seemed alarmed by this news and eager to share it, but as he looked from us to the happy colleagues on his table, I think he sensed that his hope of returning there was becoming a distant dream. Yet, despite our best efforts, he made a run for it and so we busied ourselves mingling with the other partygoers. Then it dawned on me that I'd given him bum advice. I'd completely forgotten that this new Megastore was in a brand-new location up by the Concert Hall and I had been thinking of the old store when I was mouthing off about it. This error had to be remedied and I prowled the party until I was able to tap him on the shoulder and, in words that would have made sense had I put them in the correct order, explain my mistake.

He looked at me, realising for the first time perhaps that I was not part of his happy empire; I was a worthless gate-crasher. His next words were crushing and seemed to signal that the New York job was no longer on the cards.

'You are so drunk,' he told me, 'that you are now arguing with yourself.'

At that point I felt a firm hand on my shoulder and assumed he had given some coded nod to security. Instead, it was one of my colleagues, pushing past me so he, too, could have another word with the great man.

'Richard, we're out of wine again. Would you mind doing the honours?'

To his credit, he did.

19.

LOSING THE PLOT

My father's final days, up to and including his funeral, were not short of surreal and comic moments. At the age of ninety-two, having survived everything from imprisonment as a teenager in a Siberian labour camp to a 1969 Vauxhall Viva – he always said the latter was the worst of those ordeals – he had finally expired in a nursing home in the East End of Glasgow. He had been in that home for just the last five months of his life, having resisted my various attempts to coax him into sheltered housing or a care home. I had told him that either of those would be safer than the split-level ex-council house he had lived in since 1973.

Unpersuaded he had, instead, made his own adaptations to the house so that he could climb the four flights of stairs. His days in the navy had equipped him with a sailor's knowledge of ropes and pulleys and he had rigged these around the staircases in a snook-cocking, low-budget alternative to Stannah stairlifts.

The start of his tenth decade, however, was characterised by frequent stays in hospital and it became part of my twice-weekly routine to walk from Pacific Quay to the Glasgow Royal Infirmary, grabbing a fish supper en route, then playing that game of Find-the-Patient as they moved him from various departments and to different wards. More than once my search had been fruitless because he had signed himself out of hospital and flagged down a taxi on the street to get himself home.

In his final months, though he told me that his adventures were coming to an end, he was still able to charm staff at the nursing home, telling the young nurses stories of his life at sea and, somewhat optimistically, signing up for cookery classes. You need to have sampled my father's cooking to see the irony there and to wonder why this had not occurred to him years earlier.

Just weeks after Christmas, he began to fade. When I got the call from the nursing home, I had been backstage at the City Halls. I had given my opening speech at the Young Traditional Musician Final, promising the audience I would be back in under three hours to announce the winner. After that call, I left the building and caught a taxi, wondering if I would get to Dad's bedside in time. As it turned out, he would slip in and out of consciousness for another few hours and, by morning, many other family members were able to be there for him. As the light started to stream into his room, he seemed to wake a little. I squeezed his hand and told him that we were all there and that everything was all right. Then he was gone.

Ten days later, the family gathered at the crematorium. In the winter months, the Reaper was busy with his scythe, so the funeral services had to be conducted speedily, as a hearse drew up every fifteen or thirty minutes. I shuffled onto the front pew alongside Anne, my sister Rose and my six brothers. We had booked a civil celebrant and given him an outline script with information about Dad's early life as a farm labourer, his escape from the Nazis, his capture by the Russians and his service on a battleship escorting North Atlantic convoys. We omitted references to the failings of Vauxhall cars.

As we waited for the celebrant to take his place out front, I looked behind me to see who else had turned up to bid Dad a final farewell. Of course, I recognised my brothers' wives and children, a few neighbours, nursing staff. But who were the forty or so other strangers who had crammed into the back benches? Former shipmates? That was unlikely as Dad had outlived most of them. Members of the Polish Club? Perhaps, I reasoned, Dad had made more friends than we knew in the last years of his life. But then there was a kerfuffle at the door and our civil celebrant seemed to be having a heated discussion with a church minister about who should step forward to the rostrum. Our man won and his first announcement that 'This was the funeral of Frank Zycinski' produced an eruption of groans and mutterings from the back of the hall and, as a unit, the forty strangers stood up and left.

Wrong funeral, guys.

At the end of the service, we in the front row filed down to the door and lined up to shake hands with other mourners, thank them for their attendance and remind them there was a drink and sandwiches waiting in a local hotel should they choose to partake. It was during that line-up that a man I did not recognise – and he may well have been a straggler from the other funeral – greeted me with a firm handshake and, not in a mean-spirited way, said, 'I see Ian Rankin thinks you're a fanny.'

It was one of those moments when I heard the words but simply assumed I had misunderstood and so I nodded and smiled and moved on to the next handshake. 'Ian Rankin thinks you're a fanny' could have been my distraught ears mishearing a sentence like, 'I'm thanking you on behalf of the many'. You know ... that sentence I expect to hear when the Queen gives me a knighthood.

But it wasn't.

The following day, a discussion with the BBC Press Office confirmed that the best-selling crime author Ian Rankin did, indeed think I was a fanny and in fact he had thrown in the word 'numptie' for good measure. Maybe not me, personally, but whoever was running Radio Scotland. Now, if you're not from Scotland, you might not be aware of the local connotations surrounding such terms, but bear with me, because I now have to tell you what happened when I had to appear on Radio 4 and explain those terms to the rest of Britain.

Ian Rankin, it seemed, had got wind of some schedule changes I was planning at Radio Scotland and had taken particular exception to my plan to displace Janice Forsyth from her Saturday morning slot and create a sixth edition of our morning news show *Good Morning Scotland*. Janice had been presenting her breezy mix of chat and competitions since the days of James Boyle, but was being hammered in the ratings by Radio 2, and the *Graham Norton Show* in particular. I hadn't been planning to lose Janice completely. She was a brilliant champion of the Scottish music scene and well-connected with the artistic life of Scotland, so my ultimate plan was to double the duration of our afternoon culture show and ask Janice to present it four days a week.

Given that Radio 4 was still struggling to cover the cultural scene north of the Watford Gap, I felt Radio Scotland should devote more airtime to the arts, theatre, film, music and books. As is always the way with schedule changes, this plan would impact on other programmes and presenters, so had to remain under wraps until I had spoken to everyone involved. Although the Saturday morning changes had leaked out, I hadn't been able to assure listeners that Janice would remain and, indeed, would become a bigger part of the new schedule. Also, organising Dad's funeral had kept me out of the office for more than a week, so the BBC Scotland Press Office didn't have the facts to deal with the queries.

Into this vacuum stepped Janice superfan, Ian Rankin, who had penned a poem on the issue which he had read aloud at one of those meet-the-author events. Now, I'm too tight-fisted to pay the copyright, so I won't print the whole poem here (you can Google it for yourself), but as hitherto explained, it referred to the management of BBC Radio Scotland as a bunch of fannies and numpties ... which brings me to Radio 4 and the weekly *Feedback* programme presented by Roger Bolton.

This is the show where listeners to BBC Radio get the chance to ask questions of the people who run the radio stations. It's mostly devoted to complaints about Radio 4 or the other BBC UK networks, but occasionally we in the Nations and Regions get to wander onto the airwaves and say stuff. I have been a guest on *Feedback* a handful of times and even appeared live with Roger at the Edinburgh Fringe, when the production company decided to take the show on the road and record an episode in the BBC Festival tent. This time, however, I was sitting in the contribution studio in Glasgow as Roger was recording the interview in London. As ever, while we were setting levels and testing the line, Roger asked me how to pronounce my name and that led to a discussion about its origins, my dad's life and Roger's own encounters with Polish ex-servicemen in Scotland. Then we got the word from the producer that we were good to go and Roger's first question.

'What's a fanny?'

Before I could formulate an answer, he contextualised the question by telling his listeners about the Rankin poem and its inclusion of the words 'fanny' and 'numptie'. He asked me to define both and, while I joked that he might not be able to use the answers, I played it safe by saying that the terms could be used interchangeably to describe an idiot, a dimwit, a fool.

But then came his next question.

'Do you feel hurt by it?'

It was an oddly personal question and not one I would have expected. Maybe there was something in the tremor of my voice as I spoke to him that made him ask it, because I hadn't been hurt by Ian Rankin's criticism or his bad poetry; it had been the preamble chat about my dad that had me welling up. I realise now that I hadn't had time to absorb the events of his death; I had been too eager to get back to work and deal with daft press enquiries about the supposed axing of a beloved presenter who, in fact, was being offered a lucrative deal to stay with the station and actually do a lot more than she had been doing in the past.

Of course, I couldn't say that on *Feedback,* so I ended up muttering something feeble and unconvincing about admiring Ian Rankin's work and being disappointed with his criticism. Roger thanked me and, on Friday night, I listened to hear how my interview had been edited: all references to fannies had been cut out and only my waffle remained.

When you lose your parent – and I don't think it matters what age you are when it happens – it's a moment when you pause to take stock of life. I was now approaching my fifties and Anne and I would soon be the classic empty-nesters, each having to find a role beyond that of Mum and Dad. That in turn made me think of all the bath times and bedtimes I had missed by working late in the office or else climbing on and off trains between Glasgow and Inverness. I thought of how, even on the morning of my father's death, I had been on the phone to my PA, leaving a message about the title of Jo Caulfield's new conversation series. None of this seemed to matter anymore.

How many times had I skipped those Wednesday night visits to Dad because there had been something more important to be attended to? How important did those things seem now? That daft poem? Once I would have laughed and brushed it aside, but now such criticism made me resentful and keen to lash out. When the historian Tom Devine called for my resignation because he only liked some of the programmes on the station, I didn't smile and shake my head as I once would have done. Instead, I felt sulky and angry and keen to burst into a live studio and give him a piece of my mind.

Wisely, the Press Office determined that my boss, Donalda MacKinnon, would be better placed to give a more considered response. That's the thing about grief: when you are going through the bereavement process you might not be aware of it. Looking back now, I remember feeling disengaged from anything to do with radio. I no longer saw creative challenges, just more demands for budget savings and requests to write strategy papers which, I knew, would lead nowhere. I began to feel physically sick at the thought of climbing on a train and anxious about every meeting in my diary. I tried to ignore those palpitations in my chest, but I saw dark omens everywhere. On one train journey I felt something sticking to my shoe and reached down to remove it. It was a playing card: the ace of spades, I swear it was. It reminded me of that meeting with the tarot card reader way back in Selkirk. It had been a team night out and I had been the annoying cynic in the group. All I could remember from that reading was the man telling me that I should 'listen to my body'. Maybe it was time to see a doctor.

I made an appointment with Doctor Freda, the GP at my local surgery. She wired me up to some machinery and told me my heart was fine, but my blood pressure was high and that was undoubtedly because I had put on so much weight. How much weight? Well, in the space of twelve months, I had gained fifty pounds and gone up several waist and collar sizes. I honestly hadn't been aware of it, but when the doctor asked me to explain, I remembered all those fish suppers on the way to see Dad in hospital; the cheeseburgers and pints at Queen Street Station while waiting for a train; the Twixes and Kit Kats from the catering trolley; that time at the Radio Festival in Salford when my feet had been so sore that I could barely make the short journey from my hotel to the conference venue; being disappointed that Marks & Spencer no longer stocked a jacket in my size. It all seemed obvious now.

Too mean to join a gym, I decided to walk my weight away. There's a very steep hill near where I live in Inverness; an old military road, built after the Jacobite risings. It leads past modern housing developments and into Daviot Wood and Drumossie Moor. On my first attempt, I barely made it a few hundred yards before stopping for breath. The following day I made it a little further. By the end of the week I had made it to the top of the hill. By the end of the month I had lost one stone. By the second month I had lost another. I cut out sugary nonsense from my diet and settled for just a glass or two of red wine every few weeks. The weight fell off. To keep me distracted while walking, I listened to recordings of plays from our drama department and then downloaded some audio books: John Grisham, Michael Connelly, Stephen King. King's book *On Writing* inspired me to have a go at penning my own novel, as another possible activity to distract me from the fridge and frying pan.

Each time I returned from my walk, I would sit down and bash out 2,000 words of my story about a Hollywood agent who returned to his native Scotland in search of an old flame and ended up running a tiny radio station in the Highlands. I called it *The Good Listeners* and, encouraged by my friend, the journalist Eamonn O'Neill, decided to send it to an agent. Not knowing where to begin, I wandered into WHSmith in Inverness and looked at the bestsellers to see if there was one that might be similar to my style and story.

I landed upon one of Jenny Colgan's comedic romances and found out her agent was a woman called Ali Gunn. I contacted Ali and she told me to send her my manuscript. Two weeks later I got the following email: 'Jeff, I LOVE LOVE LOVE IT.'

She followed up a few days later with, 'I LOVE IT. WE WANT TO TAKE IT ON. I may need to give some feedback but yes, yes, yes. xx'

I was astonished. I had expected to do the rounds of agents and publishers before stuffing the novel in a drawer or slapping it up on the Amazon Kindle site for free. Instead, Ali invited me to a meeting in London and we got together up at the Bluebird Restaurant in Chelsea. She was full of praise and enthusiasm and told me my story had still made her laugh on a second reading. She spoke to me about deals she had done for other authors, some of which had involved so much money that those authors had had to leave the country for tax reasons.

She made me laugh with some indiscreet stories about her friends in the Conservative Party and various fallouts with other big agencies. She warned me that she would sometimes ask an author to do several rewrites before she tried to pitch it to a publisher and that sounded good to me. As she spoke, it dawned on me that she wasn't just any old agent but was one of the biggest and most experienced in Britain.

Nevertheless, she politely asked my thoughts on whether we should tout my novel at the London or Frankfurt Book Fair. Not having the faintest idea, I left the decision to her. We agreed that she would give it some thought and, meanwhile, I would do another draft of *The Good Listeners* and add an extra 10,000 words to the story. I walked back down the King's Road with my head spinning. It would have been enough just to get some positive feedback and encouragement to keep writing, but now Ali was suggesting life-changing deals.

I went home and continued my routine of walking and writing. Another month, another stone lost and then another. In total I had lost more than sixty pounds in less than six months. My blood pressure was back to normal and I had a lot more energy. I also had those extra 10,000 words and had filled in a few plot holes. There had been a few more email exchanges with Ali and another meeting at her office in Mayfair, but nothing was moving very fast and I began to wonder if she had had a change of heart. Then, one Saturday morning, a friend texted me with a news story he had spotted online.

> Literary agent Ali Gunn has died suddenly
> while in Switzerland. Gunn, who was 45, was
> found dead on the morning of February 20th
> after suffering a brain haemorrhage ... Tributes
> have been pouring in on social media. Among
> Gunn's authors was Jenny Colgan, who tweeted
> about her 'darling friend and fabulous agent'.

I was shocked and then sad when thinking of the times her emails had referred to her young son. I hadn't known her well and wouldn't have claimed her as a friend, but she was one of those people whose energy and enthusiasm was infectious. I sent my condolences to her business partner and it was clear everyone was stunned. That bloody Reaper had been busy again.

Then, almost as suddenly as it had started, my enthusiasm for the life of a novelist simply evaporated. I was glad to have completed an entire novel, but writing books was always something I had imagined doing in my retirement years, if only for my own pleasure. Although I had fallen temporarily out of love with radio, writing fiction had satisfied my need to be doing something creative. Now, with Ali gone, I had no stomach for touting my book around different agencies, and as I looked at the bestsellers in WHSmith, I could see that the market had moved on to crime fiction and serial killers. Perhaps one day I would resurrect Nelson S. Pipsqueak as a hard-bitten sleuth.

In the meantime, I still had a radio station to run and I had to get my head back in gear.

20.

ALL TALK

Doctor Freda seemed pleased to see me.

'You're our star patient,' she told me. 'All the nurses are talking about your weight loss ... and your blood pressure is right out of the danger zone. It's amazing.'

'I just followed your advice: diet, exercise, cut down on the booze.'

'That's what's amazing,' she said. 'No one ever listens to that advice. And how are your feet?'

'They're great,' I said. 'I've been walking for miles, at least 10,000 steps a day. Sometimes double that.'

'Again, amazing.' She paused. 'So why have you come to see me?'

'Well, I think I'm losing my mind. And since you've helped me with everything else, I thought you might help me with this.'

Those were the exact words I used. But of course, falling back on my psychology degree, I couldn't resist a bit of self-diagnosis. I described my symptoms: I felt disengaged, distracted; I had the constant worry that something dreadful was going to happen. There was no reason for this. On the face of it, life was good, but these emotions were on the verge of becoming debilitating and interfering with my ability to do my job. Doctor Freda gave me a form to complete. There was a question about how often, if ever, I had contemplated suicide. I hadn't. When I returned it to her, she totted up the scores and pronounced that I had, maybe, a bit of mild depression, but nothing serious. A mid-life crisis, perhaps.

I made a joke about life in the BBC: something about not having to be mad to work there, but how it improved your chances of promotion. Then I got a bit serious. Maybe it had something to do with my father's death, I suggested; a symptom of prolonged bereavement, perhaps? If I could impress Doctor Freda with my intellectual analysis of the situation it would prove that I wasn't as much of a fruitcake as those unfortunate souls who turned up without those four years of psychology study to help explain their neurosis. Doctor Freda scribbled out a name and phone number on a piece of paper and handed it to me.

'I think you should see someone. A specialist. Her name's Gayle.'

Gayle turned out to be a cognitive therapist and Doctor Freda explained that I could have three sessions with her courtesy of the NHS, but if my problems were more serious I would have to go on a long waiting list for further help. I have to admit, I liked the idea of telling people I had a therapist, like I was a character in a Woody Allen movie. This, however, was not Manhattan: Gayle's consulting room was housed in a spare office within a dental practice just next to the Aldi supermarket.

In our first session, she asked me to indulge in one of my favourite pastimes – talking about myself. I told Gayle about my family life, Sarah being accepted for university, Alan passing exams at school, about my dad's death, my weight loss, the novel I had written and the encouraging words from Ali Gunn. I talked about life at the BBC, about how the radio station was doing well and in fact, everything was going so well that I now felt guilty for being there at all and wasting her time. I imagined she would have much more serious cases to deal with: young mums with post-natal depression, post-war trauma victims and the like. When I finished, my mouth was dry and Gayle was admonishing my apologies.

'It's clearly serious enough for you to look for help,' she told me. 'I think this is all very interesting. I already have a theory about what's happened to you,' she teased, 'but I'll talk to you about that in two weeks. One thing I will say, though: I don't think it is all to do with your dad's death.'

That was the way it was with Gayle. She always left you on a cliff-hanger. Two weeks later I was back in her office, dodging past the people with bleeding gums, and telling her all was well.

'I feel like a million dollars,' I told her honestly. 'In fact, I felt that way as soon as I left you last time. Did you put something in the water?'

Gayle smiled. She wasn't surprised.

'People always say that. It's only because I let you talk.'

It was true. Sure, I was no stranger to talking about myself but when in a conversation with a friend, even a close friend, there's a certain amount of information-trading that has to go on for the sake of politeness. I could tell a friend about how bad I was feeling, but eventually they would feel the need to tell me something about themselves. It came back to that thing about the two halves of a conversation: one half is about talking; the other half isn't listening, it's about waiting to talk.

What Gayle had allowed me to do was just talk without interruptions and, frankly, without having to give a rat's arse about what someone else had experienced. It dawned on me that her 'talking therapy' was no different from the technique I had used to persuade people to share stories with me for the radio. Gayle noted my happy mood, but warned it might not last.

'I've been thinking a lot about your situation and trying to figure out what's going on.'

She asked me a few more questions about my job, my weight loss and the eight years I had spent travelling and living in hotels. Then she hit me with her theory. She told me that I had probably been unhappy for some time and that I had been overeating to make myself feel better. Once I quit stuffing my face, the unhappiness came to the surface. And the unhappiness was nothing to do with bereavement; it was to do with my lifestyle – all the travelling, the hotel stays and the lack of any permanency in Glasgow. She quoted something back to me that I had barely remembered telling her: 'When you live out of hotel rooms in Glasgow or Edinburgh, you don't really live there. You can't even join the sodding library.'

Gayle thought she might have the solution, but for that, I would have to wait another two weeks.

A fortnight later and Gayle revealed all: she told me I needed to have two important conversations – one with Anne and one with my boss. I needed to limit my travelling and avoid lonely hotel rooms. She suggested I get myself a permanent base in Glasgow so that I could have a proper social life there and, when the kids went to university, it would be a place for them to come round and have tea.

I was doubtful.

'But won't I just end up living a double life?'

Gayle looked at me smiling. 'I hate to break this to you, Jeff, but you are already leading a double life. Trouble is, you're not enjoying it.'

Anne jumped at the idea of us having a base in Glasgow and, though we would be a bit out of pocket with council tax costs and so on, it would allow us to be closer to the kids in an emergency. My boss liked the idea of me being closer to the main production teams in Glasgow, at least for a year.

By the end of the summer I had rented a bedsit – sorry, a *studio apartment* – within walking distance of Queen Street train station and, sure enough, when Sarah began her first term at university, we had a regular date for tea.

Now, I'd love to tell you that was me sorted, but the truth is I didn't start to get my head back in gear until the night I was invited to speak to students at Glasgow Caledonian University. This, in the days when it was known as Glasgow Tech, was where I had gained my degree. The invitation had come, not from lecturers on the Media course, but from the manager of the student radio station, Radio

Caley. James McGuire had asked me to come along and talk about my own career and offer tips on how to get a job in radio.

Afterwards I joined a group of them for a drink and a chat in a strange basement pub called the Flying Duck. Their enthusiasm was infectious and reminded me of the things I loved about radio. I stayed in touch with that small group, James, Amie Igoe, Gavin Knight, Connor Gillies and others, and offered advice and mock interviews as they applied for jobs. When Amie won one of the university's prestigious Magnusson grants, I was able to help her put together a week of work experience in New York, linking her up with my old friend from Cardiff, Heather Bosch, at CBS. James became the breakfast show producer at Capital Radio in Glasgow. Gavin went to work for STV's political team. Connor became an award-winning news reporter at Heart and is now at BBC News, and Amie became a producer on the *Kaye Adams* team at Radio Scotland.

The next boost came when I was able to tempt an old rival to join my management team. Back in 2006, Colin Paterson had been appointed programme director of Talk 107, a new speech station based in Edinburgh. Weeks before the launch, Colin invited me for lunch and, despite knowing that we would soon be competing for listeners, I liked him immediately. We had similar backgrounds – he had grown up in Larkhall – and although he was fifteen years younger than me, he had an air of confidence and maturity and spoke candidly about the challenges he faced. With a limited budget for presenters, he had tried to woo the talent by offering them more than just money. One famous broadcaster was known to have an interest in the environment, so he offered to power Talk 107 with a wind turbine if she would come on board. She didn't. When his station hit the airwaves, the press came calling for a quote and I offered words of congratulation. This was in stark contrast to the brutal comments made by Colin's counterparts in the commercial sector. In the end, Talk 107, despite its on-air swagger, struggled to find enough listeners in the tightly defined transmission area dictated by its licence. Before Colin moved on, I decided to return the favour and invited him for dinner in a fairly posh restaurant in Edinburgh. Over candlelight, we raised a glass of fine wine to future adventures and traded anecdotes about eccentric presenters and plans that had gone awry.

Things started to heat up when, somehow, the candle flame set light to my napkin and began to scorch the tablecloth. A waiter arrived to avert a disaster. He killed the fire, but a pall of black smoke now hung over the restaurant and you could hear coughing and spluttering at nearby tables. Colin had almost gone out in a blaze of glory, but he popped up a few years later as the Deputy Editor of BBC Radio Wales. I saw him regularly at BBC meetings and our friendship developed.

In 2014, there were two big events in Scotland: the Commonwealth Games in Glasgow and then the referendum on Scottish independence. The Games prompted a reshuffle of responsibilities at BBC Scotland and created a vacancy for the editor in charge of Radio Scotland's topical programmes and events. I asked Colin to apply and there was much heartbreak in Wales when he got the job and moved back to Scotland.

As teams from BBC Sport arrived en masse to prepare coverage of the Games, Colin got to grips with his radio portfolio. He created a pop-up radio station – *Commonwealth Voices* – that would be based at the Forge Shopping Centre, across the street from the Emirates Stadium in Parkhead. This would offer yet another training opportunity for local media students and link us with radio stations around the Commonwealth. Colin also took editorial control of the *Kaye Adams Programme* and the afternoon arts show. It's fair to say there were those among our production staff who were wary of this thirty-something whizz kid with his background in commercial stations, but he had an instinctive feel for good radio, set specific targets for programme-makers and wasn't afraid to tell me if I had made a mistake or if it was time to say goodbye to presenters who were no longer pulling their weight.

Sharing the load with Colin meant I had time to talk to other people about new programme ideas. A coffee chat with Eamonn O'Neill, the investigative reporter turned lecturer, prompted me to commission him to make a series about the intelligence services in Scotland and beyond. This developed into a season called *Secrets and Spies*, which included a historical documentary from Billy Kay, while Robbie Coltrane presented a fun programme on James Bond's Scottish credentials, *Licensed to Kilt*.

I also resurrected an idea that I had been trying to make real for a number of years. Given that so many radio formats are based on the kind of conversations people have in real situations – think how the late Anthony Clare had hosted Radio 4's *In the Psychiatrist's Chair*, or how Father Joe Mills had presented Radio Scotland's *Comedy Confessions*

– I had always wanted to mimic the elements of a police interrogation and have a celebrity guest subjected to questioning from real detectives doing the old nasty and nice routine. I had floated the title *Good Cop, Bad Cop* among many producers and now the Features team in Edinburgh had managed to track down two retired CID officers who were willing to try their hand at presenting radio programmes. But who, I was asked, should be the first victim of this double-act? Who should they subject to a half-hour of questions that alternated between encouragement and accusation? Who could cope with being asked soft-ball queries about their successes and then have to handle sneering remarks about their need for attention? It could end up being quite an ordeal for any guest willing to sweat it out. Torture, even.

When the producer suggested the crime writer, Ian Rankin, I thought he would be perfect.

21.

YES AND NO

It was Friday, 19th September 2014, and, just hours after Scotland had voted to stay part of the United Kingdom, I was back in Glasgow's George Square. It was still called that, although, had the vote gone the other way, there had been talk of renaming it 'Independence Square'. I had often crossed the square during the many weeks of the referendum campaign because it was adjacent to Queen Street station, my home from home during the years I commuted to Inverness, Edinburgh and Aberdeen. In those cities, you got very different impressions of how the vote might go.

One night, after threading my way through the crowds to catch a train, I arrived at Edinburgh's Waverley Station and saw one cheerful, middle-aged woman who, with leaflets in her hand, I initially mistook for a Jehovah's Witness. But no, this was the full force of the 'Better Together' campaign in action.

In Aberdeen, you could take the political temperature via conversations with taxi drivers. Many bemoaned the city's economic downturn because of the falling price of oil (although whether that was going to make them vote 'Yes' or 'No' was never obvious). One driver gave me a little blue booklet compiled by the pro-independence *Wings Over Scotland* website. He told me he had been giving these to all his passengers because they needed to know the truth. I'm not sure how this impacted on his tips.

In Inverness, campaigning seemed to be confined to the pedestrian precinct on the High Street. At one end there would be a stall for the 'Yes' campaign, where a costumed actor portraying Robert the Bruce would sometimes appear; at the other end of the street was the 'Better Together' stall handing out their 'No Thanks' lapel stickers. My daughter, Sarah, with no other thought than her Saturday shopping list, committed a bit of a faux pas when she refused the offer of a pro-independence leaflet with a polite 'No thanks' and was then pursued along the street by an elderly 'Yes' supporter loudly questioning her patriotism.

Dundee, people said, was veering towards 'Yes', but not the Angus coast.

Glasgow had always looked and felt like a 'Yes' city. The saltires and 'Yes' flags seemed to be everywhere, far outnumbering the occasional 'Naw' stickers I spotted on lampposts. For most of those weeks, the atmosphere in George Square had been joyful, with independence campaigners, young and old, anticipating a victory celebration. True, on meeting an old friend from my student days, she had joked that George Square would also be where they would build the gallows to 'string up you lot from the

BBC', but that had been before the attacks on 'BBC bias' had really got going and such remarks could still provoke a laugh, or a thin smile.

That day after the result, events in George Square revealed something about how trust in the BBC had eroded among the pro-independence campaigners. I had arranged to meet Sarah after her final university lecture of the day and we had booked a table for dinner in a nearby restaurant. There were still dozens of saltires on display and plenty of people keen to show that the 'No' vote had not dampened their enthusiasm. Suddenly there was a blare of horns as a convoy of cars came alongside the City Chambers and was stopped by police at the corner of the square. As these cars disgorged their occupants, it became clear that these were pro-Union supporters, many of them carrying banners about the Orange Order alongside the Union flags. There was an immediate stand-off between this group and those who had been in the square.

The happy scene changed rapidly. From side streets came more police, some on horseback, to swell the ranks of those who had already been patrolling. They managed to separate the two groups, although the margin of no-man's land between them was little more than arm's length, and the chants and shouts from each side became louder by the minute. The new arrivals were singing a ditty called 'Stick your independence up your arse,' which was not particularly melodic.

I called the BBC newsroom in Glasgow and got through to our Radio News Editor. He told me that *Reporting Scotland* TV reporter Cameron Buttle was nearby, and, sure enough, Cameron arrived and, within minutes, BBC Scotland was reporting the scene live on radio and on BBC 1. With my phone, I took pictures for our online sites. More police arrived and, by the end of that night, a wider cordon had been established, with Union supporters bottled up beside the train station.

I mention this because these were events that I had witnessed for myself and not through the media. Yet an odd thing happened after that. For a time, it was part of the folk-lore of the 'biased BBC' that we had not reported this incident at all, or that, by including a description of the incident in a wider online story about the referendum result, we had made a concerted effort to bury it. 'Bias by omission' was a claim that plagued us in radio and television throughout the campaign.

From the outset we knew we would be in the firing line and we expected there would be complaints from all quarters. At BBC Scotland, a special hotline was set up so that campaign chiefs from 'Yes' and 'Better Together' had a fast and direct means of getting in touch if they had a legitimate concern.

Each day, editorial heads from radio, television and online sat in a morning meeting, to discuss our coverage and flag up any issues that were likely to cause problems in the next 24 hours. Often these discussions centred on terminology or the composition of studio panels. One of my main talking points throughout that period was about the number of Radio Scotland presenters who were itching to play an active part in the campaign but felt the BBC guidelines on impartiality were restricting their freedom of speech.

Social media proved to be our biggest problem, and I don't think there's any doubt that BBC Scotland was not geared up to respond to the various accusations thrown at us on Facebook and Twitter. We struggled to respond to articles on sites such as *Wings Over Scotland*, which, for a one-man operation, displayed a remarkable propensity for finding data and shareable memes and graphs to bolster the cause of independence and take swipes at the mainstream media for, in its view, burying the truth.

Presenters like Gary Robertson and Kaye Adams were also subjected to some pretty nasty personal attacks, but we took the view that to make some of this known would, in itself, become a news story that might be seen as partisan. Where we really fell down, I believe, is in the speed of our response when accused of not covering a particular claim from one side of the campaign or another. In most cases we had, but the complainant had not heard or seen it.

When Kaye Adams began a series of daily interviews with campaign leaders, listeners who had only heard one of those programmes were outraged that there was no balancing view from the other side. BBC News online created more confusion, since the underlying algorithms allowed stories to rise in prominence, depending not just on how recently they had been posted, but on how many people had viewed them. It was difficult to explain to the campaign chiefs that, yes, we had covered their claim or counterclaim, that it had appeared on the News online website and was still there, but that it had fallen from prominence because not enough people found it interesting.

For the BBC, the biggest flashpoint came when more network reporters arrived from London in the last weeks of the referendum campaign, just as the polls were suggesting that a victory for the 'Yes' side was in sight. For anyone down south who doubted that things might be about to change, this was big news, and no wonder that the big-gun reporters from TV and newspapers arrived en masse to cover it.

The BBC's Nick Robinson had his infamous clash with Alex Salmond. Nick's television report had suggested that the SNP leader had not answered the BBC's question during a press conference. In fact, he *had* answered it, but clearly not to Nick Robinson's satisfaction. Evidence of bias or just sloppy reporting? Either way, not good enough. Even before that, though, it was clear that colleagues from London were picking up some old chestnuts and resurrecting angles of the story that had already been laid to rest by reporters in Scotland. Issues such as the need for separate passports in an independent Scotland were being discussed again, instead of the real meat of the story, which was about the economic consequences of independence and the future relationship with Europe. News reporters also tended to talk about the things that *might* change, rather than the consequences of the status quo, and that created its own imbalance.

What astonished me in the months before the campaign was how senior radio colleagues in London seemed so ill-informed about the political climate in Scotland. As the day of the vote drew closer, they would ask me to predict the result, or brazenly ask how I was going to vote myself. I declined to answer. There were some jokes about how I could apply to be Director General of a Scottish Broadcasting Corporation. It was obvious they thought a 'Yes' vote was unlikely.

It was only as the polls narrowed that the topic was properly discussed at the UK Radio Board and, as I joined the meeting via a video conference from Inverness, I felt like shouting 'So, now you're interested!' into the camera. Even then, though, there was no question of the BBC trying to manipulate public opinion, just some journalistic salivation at the thought of an exciting week of news coverage. Oh, and one brief mention from the new Director of Radio, Helen Boaden, who pointed out how much of the BBC's budget came from licence-fee payers in Scotland. Finally, after all my rants about network spend in Scotland, the penny was dropping.

It was a social-media post from *The Daily Record's* Paul English who first alerted me to the thousands of protestors about to descend on our HQ in Glasgow. He had seen them march past his office window at Anderston Quay and had posted 'Wow!' as he saw the line of protestors stretch along the banks of the Clyde and the placards calling for the sacking of Nick Robinson. The letters 'BBC' now represented the 'Biased Broadcasting Corporation', and so forth. The organisers described the event as good-natured and joyous. Those inside the building felt less joyous about it. It was not quite pitchforks and flaming torches, but it was not the day to nip out for a sandwich.

I have often wondered about the timing of that protest and whether it did more harm than good for the 'Yes' campaign. With opinion polls suggesting that the tipping point had almost been reached and supporters of the Union might be about to change sides, had that highly visible attack on the BBC prevented that final flip?

As much as many of the 'Yes' side had now convinced themselves that we were a force for evil, actual trust levels in the BBC were still higher than for any other media organisation. If you needed a good slice of those BBC-believers to become 'Yes' voters, I don't think a march on our studios – televised on our own news programmes, as well as on CNN and Russia Today – was the way to convince them. But what do I know?

I was part of the mainstream media conspiracy and I'd played devil's advocate so often that Lucifer had me on a retainer. Whenever a friend or colleague offered strong opinions about a particular subject, my natural instinct was to take an alternative point of view, just to test out their logic. On the rare occasions I could convince them to see it my way, I then switched sides and argued the opposite case. During the referendum campaign, such mental horseplay was a good way to lose friends.

On the night of the results, I was in Pacific Quay and it soon became clear which way the wind was blowing. Planned TV and radio appearances from the pro-independence side were being cancelled, and when Ruth Davidson, the Tory leader in Scotland, appeared, she was all smiles.

Of those who had voted, 45 per cent wanted independence, and 55 per cent did not. The turnout was an astonishing 85 per cent.

Regardless of the result, Scotland had changed, and in our news and speech programmes we could track the growing engagement of listeners in politics and the issues that had been thrown up by the campaign: tax, currency, health, education, immigration, trade and Europe. Having made temporary schedule changes to reflect listeners' appetite for discussion and analysis, I felt it would be a mistake if Radio Scotland didn't follow through.

I sat down with Colin Paterson and we mapped out a new daytime schedule which would allow for an extra

Sunday edition of *Good Morning Scotland*, and for Kaye Adams to present a three-hour format that would include an hour-long phone-in after nine and then a sequence of interviews and human-interest stories until noon. It was an opportunity to make other changes, too. Colin was particularly keen that we put real effort into our social-media strategy, and we removed this burden from the remit of our website team and asked Lizzy Clark and James Christie to learn all the dos and don'ts of these platforms and give us a real connection with listeners on Facebook and Twitter.

Our social-media figures rose dramatically. From just a few thousand followers on Facebook, the Radio Scotland page began to gain 5,000 new followers a week, outstripping many of the BBC's UK radio stations. The Scottish news and political landscape was now ripe for satire and we needed a vehicle for that. I handed our comedy and topical teams no more than the title *Breaking the News* and they came up with the format that would be presented by Des Clarke and go on to win numerous awards.

Thinking back to the Commonwealth Games, and how BBC Sport had used the reception foyer at PQ for a nightly TV chat show, I asked our music team to create something similar for the new schedule. Barbara Wallace and Mandy Freeman were excited by the prospect of a live music show in front of an audience, and Sharon Mair, as she took up a new role in charge of radio's music output, developed her 'pass the hat' strategy and found money from different BBC departments to ensure that the show would have a presence beyond radio. Cameras and lighting gave us content for our own website, as well as on the *BBC Introducing* site and then on BBC 2 Scotland television as a monthly compilation show.

The show would be called *The Quay Sessions* and we had no real guarantee that bands and artists would want to take part, but I commissioned it for thirty weeks of the year and crossed my fingers.

'Build it and they will come,' I told Barbara and Mandy and come they did. *The Quay Sessions*, alongside Kaye's new format and then *Breaking the News*, became three immediate success stories of the new schedule. The Inverness team revamped our weekly science show, *Brainwaves*, and Gillian Russell presented *Personal Best* in a format created by Suzy Beaumont that reflected the audience interest in health, fitness and personal development.

As I said before, when you start changing one part of the schedule, it impacts other areas, so we asked Demus Productions to launch a new late-night music show, *The Music Match*, as an entry point for new presentation talent and, in particular, female presenters.

The new programmes bedded in quickly, and there were surprisingly few complaints about the shows and the presenters we had had to lose to clear space in the schedule. Once again, the listening figures were climbing. I felt we had given a good boost to both our speech and our music formats, but became more convinced than ever that our programme ambitions couldn't be achieved unless we created an additional radio station for Scotland.

It was time for yet another strategy paper.

22.

IN THE ZONE

Within weeks of me taking the reins at BBC Radio Scotland, there had been another strike. The two events were not connected. This was pan-BBC industrial action by journalists. Morale in the newsroom was at rock bottom etc. On the street outside our Queen Margaret Drive HQ, the local NUJ chapel had organised a small rally and invited local politicians to make some speeches and show solidarity. I could hear some of this as I sat in my new and absurdly huge office with its corner view of the Botanic Gardens.

The newsroom walkout had forced me to fill gaps in the Radio Scotland schedule left by the absence of *Good Morning Scotland* and *Newsdrive*. I had chosen back-to-back episodes of a series exploring the social and political changes happening in South Africa. It was serious stuff – newsy – and, more importantly, it filled the airtime. Our Investigations Reporter, Bob Wylie, had presented the series and was one of the journalists now outside on the picket line. Glasgow MSP Pauline McNeill had come along to voice her support and there was cheer after cheer as she told the crowd how they had been right to take action, that their work was important to the people of Scotland and that you simply couldn't live without programmes like *Good Morning Scotland.*

'I was listening to Radio Scotland on the drive here,' she told the strikers, 'and you want to hear the rubbish they've had to put on because you are not at work.'

Bob was taken aback, and I'm told his feeble shout of 'I didnae think it was that bad' was drowned out by the applause of his comrades.

There was, however, a silver lining to that strike because as we had scoured the Radio Scotland archive of tapes to plug holes in the schedule, an opportunity presented itself. My colleague Sharon Mair had been finding these alternatives to news programmes and, not knowing if the strike would be prolonged or might spread to other departments, she had found a week's worth of material which she had stored in our old Dalet computerised playout system. It was at this point she mentioned, almost as an aside, that the system could be programmed to play itself if no one was around to press the buttons. The term for this was 'running wild'. I loved the sound of that.

I looked at her as she explained all the technicalities and suddenly I remembered my trip to that little station in Coos Bay and the computer server in their reception area – the automated station that played church sermons on a loop.

'Do you mean we can automate the entire schedule?'

'In theory, yes,' said Sharon. 'Dalet's not really designed for that, but in theory you could automate the whole thing for days on end, and even schedule it from a laptop that you take home each night.'

In the end, we didn't need to do that because the dispute was resolved and the journalists went back to their desks. By the time we moved to our new riverside home at Pacific Quay, however, we had a whole new set of toys to play with. Alongside the brand-new playout system, there was a digital library to catalogue and store our archive of programmes. This was a first for the BBC. All the old tapes and spools that had been crammed into shelves in the basement were now being converted to digital files and loaded onto computer storage systems. You could search for any previously broadcast radio programme using a simple bit of software on your desktop computer. This made the possibility of an automated station all the more feasible and I was keen to try it out. The annual Children in Need appeal gave me the excuse we needed and I asked Senior Producer, Lizzy Clark, to take charge of a project we called BBC Radio Pudsey.

Cumbersome rules laid down by the BBC Trust meant that any new BBC service required a lengthy approval process and, for fear of market impact, no programmes could be broadcast online unless they had already been transmitted on an existing BBC radio station. Children in Need was different in that it was managed at arm's length from the BBC. My former colleague Gareth Hydes was now one of the top executives at Pudsey HQ and he was keen on the idea.

We would create an online radio station, available across the UK, that showcased the work of the charities funded by donations to Pudsey. We would keep things sounding lively with a cast of young presenters and famous guests. To stay within BBC rules, we would offer five hours of original content each day, but this would first be broadcast overnight on Radio Scotland's medium-wave frequency. Those five hours would then go online and be looped continually until refreshed the following day. We could monitor online traffic almost instantly and could see that the station's audience, though small, grew consistently until the big Children in Need fundraising appeal day itself, and then it tailed off. It showed us how easily we could create a brand-new radio station, despite the BBC Trust's red tape.

That led us to launch the Radio Scotland Zones: five compilations of archive content – comedy, history, new music, Celtic music and cultural programmes. Each zone would have its own Internet stream on the website and you could also tune in on one of the new Internet radio sets that were hitting the shops. You simply programmed each service into one of the pre-select buttons and fired through them one after the other, essentially showing that, in addition to BBC Radio Scotland, we now had five other services available at any one time.

Those listeners who wanted more history or traditional music programmes could press a button and find them. Listeners who didn't like sport on Saturday afternoons now had plenty of alternatives. The marketing team put together a fun television promotion showing a kitchen radio bursting open with all this extra content. Speaking to members of the Scottish Parliament, the Director General Mark Thompson said that the audio zones were an imaginative and intelligent response to one of the challenges that Radio Scotland faces:

Almost everyone I speak to is signed up to the idea that a national English-language radio station for Scotland makes a lot of sense, but radio listeners have different expectations, of course. Some people would like the station to be like a Scottish Radio 4, only more so; other people have other specialist music and cultural activity needs. Therefore, whoever runs Radio Scotland has an interesting circle to square. Trying to tease out ways in which people with different needs from those covered by Radio Scotland can easily find things that suit and work for them is an interesting aspect of audio zones. As Donalda MacKinnon said, running Radio Scotland is one of the toughest creative jobs in the entire BBC because the expectations of the audience are so complex and sometimes feel almost contradictory.

That felt like a great vote of confidence and I was further encouraged by the notion that I was doing one of the toughest creative jobs in the BBC. I made great use of that line with my television colleagues until they threatened to cut off my fruit allowance at future meetings.

Of course, as Lizzy soon found out, there was a lot more to the Zones than just dragging programmes from the library into the playout system. She booked relevant presenters to record voice tracks for each service, introducing programmes and reflecting on what they had just heard. There were copyright payments to be made and music reporting to be done, but for a small investment, we had come up with an innovative approach to radio that I hoped would grow and develop as Wi-Fi availability became the norm and when, with luck, the BBC Trust relaxed some of its rules about what content could be made available online.

Alas, not everyone saw the future through the same optimistic lens. I learned the hard way that even good ideas could be orphaned when they lost the support of the BBC's top bosses. When the next round of BBC cuts came along – under Mark Thompson's banner of *Delivering Quality First* – the Zones got the chop. Despite that, I remained convinced that the BBC needed to offer more than one English and one Gaelic radio station to the audience in Scotland. I watched, with envy and concern, the growth of brands and sub-brands in the commercial sector: Absolute Radio spawned Absolute 80s, Absolute 90s and so on; Capital Radio had Capital Gold and then Radio X. More and more people were listening to radio on smartphones and other Wi-Fi-connected devices. We were being left behind.

As the BBC began the process of seeking a new Royal Charter, I attended some initial brainstorming sessions in London and suggested that licence-payers might feel more inclined to cough up if they saw new radio services being launched. How about a dedicated comedy station, I suggested, and not just the old stuff that played on 4 Extra; a contemporary comedy station reflecting the scene all over the UK and around the world? There were polite nods but nothing more. Instead, London colleagues got behind the launch of a highbrow 'Ideas Service', which was a concept so nebulous that each person I spoke to had a different description of what it was meant to be.

Back in Scotland, the big charter idea was for a new BBC Scotland television channel which would include a home-grown programme of national and international news. As an Executive

Board we backed it to the hilt, but there were always fears that it might be under-funded or killed off completely. As a back-up strategy, I resurrected the idea of a new music and culture radio station for Scotland and, for eight days in November, 'Radio Scotland Music Extra' was piloted to an enthusiastic response from listeners and musicians. With the help of BBC Distribution, we put together a plan to have an additional radio service carried on the commercial DAB transmitters as well as online, on the BBC radio app, on satellite television and on Freeview. Everyone in Scotland would have some means of listening to the new station.

Then, to the surprise of many – including me – the idea of a BBC Scotland TV channel got the go-ahead from the Director General, Tony Hall, and it was all hands to the pump to make that happen. The new television channel became the priority and there was nervousness about diverting any new money towards radio.

Will the additional music service ever become a reality? I hope so. The radio market continues to evolve. Every week, 95 per cent of people in the UK tune in. But the time spent with radio is declining, especially in the evening, and if Radio Scotland continues to support home-grown music and culture, it needs a daytime service in addition to that offering news and sport. Podcasting is a growth area and there are some brilliant podcasts out there, but in percentage terms, podcast-downloading is tiny compared to those who still love live radio. I suspect we will see the BBC's network radio stations launch spin-off digital services targeted at specific audience groups. It would be good to see BBC Scotland get a piece of that action.

And if anyone wants to invest in a comedy station, let me know. It might be a laugh.

23.

WHEN THE CHIPS ARE DOWN

People in the BBC, like in any job, sometimes moan about their workload or having to stay late to complete a tricky edit or book guests for a show. You could sympathise, if you felt so inclined, or you could go for the reality check approach by saying, 'Yeah, that's tough, but it's not exactly like going down the mines, is it?'

If I said something like that, I could at least lay claim to actually having worked down the mines. Well, sort of. In what I now like to call my 'gap year' between school and university I took a job at Cardowan Colliery on the eastern outskirts of Glasgow. As a junior in the Wages Office, I was never at the coal face, but I did get my hands dirty transcribing the information from the shift foremen's dusty log books into a primitive card-reader computer. I can still remember the colour-coding system in those old books: a blue tick against a miner's name meant he had worked a day shift; red was for back shift; and black was for night shift. My job was to count these ticks each day and pencil the totals carefully within the printed boxes on individual data cards. Nothing I have ever done since compares to the excruciating boredom of that chore, although I bet I could now sell it to Radio Scotland's *Personal Best* programme as an exercise in mindfulness. The highlight of the week came on Wednesday afternoons when we opened external hatches in the cash office and handed over pay packets to the miners who queued outside. Many had just emerged from the pit-head showers but would still have a thin residue of coal dust around their eyes. I was rightly ridiculed when I asked curiously why so many of the workers wore eyeliner.

Cardowan Colliery also gave me my first glimpse of raw industrial action. There was a week-long strike with a sizeable picket line at the main gates, and the classic images of trucks being turned away and miners warming their hands around a flaming brazier. As a teenage office boy, I wasn't quite sure if I should cross the line or not. Thankfully, the miners took pity on me and allowed me to pass through the gates so that I could go and ask the office manager what I should do. He, in turn, sent me home. There were no ticks to count that day.

Experiences like that, alongside after-school jobs stacking shelves in a supermarket and then my time at commercial radio, gave me an acute awareness that the BBC was a relatively benign employer and a great place to work. Exhibit the slightest sniff or cough and you were actively encouraged to stay home lest you spread your filthy germs. Compare that with the story of a friend in commercial radio who once suffered a whiplash injury when driving because another car hit her from behind. Despite doctor's orders to take some recovery time, her editor called and asked, with obvious impatience, when she would be back at work. The next day she was at her desk, with the collar brace around her neck prompting comments that she was 'making a bit of a meal of it'.

The BBC's Human Resources teams were, by and large, smart people who displayed a genuine concern for the welfare of the workers. If anyone listened to the rhetoric from local union officials, though, they would get the impression that the HR department had been staffed by the Director General's evil henchmen. If anything, the HR policies were *too* caring. When job losses were announced, you could be sure that six or twelve months would be spent on genuine efforts to find redeployment opportunities for anyone at risk. During this period there would be an atmosphere of paralysis and insecurity as everyone waited to find out who would go and who would stay. It would have been a lot less painful if we had been allowed to point out the people we no longer needed, hand them a generous wad of cash and wish them '*bon voyage*' or – in a nod to the legendary revolving-door policy of redundancies and re-engagements – '*au revoir*'. Instead, the months of uncertainty within teams encouraged the people with get-up-and-go to get up and go.

Unions and bosses tended to agree that the BBC's system of performance management left a lot to be desired, but neither side could agree on the solution. One manager's attempt at straight-talking and tough love might be cited as bullying and intimidation by the union, whereas another manager's policy of gentle encouragement and numerous 'second chances' would be seen, by staff, as ineffectual shilly-shallying.

Leadership away-days often involved Lego. Having once spent Christmas Eve building a Lego version of Hogwarts Castle for Sarah (for which Santa got the damn credit!), I considered myself a bit of an expert in this field. In a course setting, however, it was all about groups of five or six colleagues deciding to apportion tasks: one might separate the bricks, one would read instructions, another would do the connecting, and so on. This seemed to me to be more about union-controlled demarcation than good productivity, but my observation earned me a strong rebuke from the external consultant.

In other courses, the BBC would try to give us techniques for dealing with disputes within teams or with poorly performing colleagues. I particularly enjoyed a series of away-day sessions held for senior staff at a very nice country hotel in Perthshire. Between top-notch meals and woodland walks, we attended workshops led by two external management coaches, each of whom had their own particular approach. Whereas one relied heavily on Buddhist philosophy and the teachings of the Dalai Lama, the other introduced us to the culture and tribal beliefs of Native Americans.

There was, as you can imagine, an element of cynicism and outright resistance from some colleagues, but I always took a pick 'n' mix approach to these away-days. Sure, some of the ideas sounded bonkers, but others were immediately useful. Not everyone appreciated standing around an imaginary tepee and thinking of their strengths and skills as the arrows in their quiver. You could wound someone with anger, I seem to recall, or pierce pomposity with your humour. Then again, the workshop on having 'Courageous Conversations' is something I have held on to. This, in a nutshell, involved tackling a thorny issue quickly and effectively. In our role-playing sessions we had laughed and cringed in recognition of failed attempts by a manager to discuss a problem with a member of staff. In a hypothetical situation, the problem employee was what might be described as a lazy, whining, pain-in-the-backside. It was comedy gold and, as we each tried to bring him onside without grabbing him by the scruff of the neck and bashing his head against a wall, there should have been individual awards for Excellence in Pussy-Footing or Beating around the Bush.

The idea of a Courageous Conversation was that, in under thirty seconds, you had to, seriously but without anger, confront an individual with a clear description of the problem. You needed evidence, preferably your own eye-witness account, to back up what you were saying, then had to explain how this behaviour was impacting on the job or on colleagues. You then offered a possible mitigation for the behaviour and allowed the person to respond so that you could begin a discussion on the right footing and find a solution. An example might be:

> Thanks for coming, Morag. I wanted to talk to
> you about your time-keeping. I've noticed that
> you've not been at your desk until half past
> nine or quarter to ten. That's causing a problem
> because the others have to cover the phones
> until you arrive. It may be that no one ever

gave you clear instructions on your hours of
duty. I wonder if that's why you've been
coming in late – in which case that's our fault –
or is it something else? (26 seconds)

Or

Good to see you, Jeff. I wanted to talk to you
about your *Behaviours* and *Values*. I notice you
drink about twenty cups of coffee a day and
that each cup involves a twenty-minute round
trip to the canteen. It may be the caffeine that
is making you short-tempered. Yesterday, I
personally saw you push a colleague from the
Gaelic department ... into the Clyde actually. It
may be you didn't get the note about how we
value Gaelic TV shows as much as the others –
in which case, that's understandable. Do you
have anything to say before the police come?
(29 seconds, not counting handcuffing)

Joking aside, it really is a good technique and one I
wished I'd been taught years ago. Yet, despite all this
investment in management and leadership skills, the BBC
always seemed to allow molehills to become mountains and
a simple bit of poor communication or a personality clash
could result in a sequence of hearings and appeals that
would drag on for years. As a leadership figure in one
department I was occasionally called upon to hear the appeal
– or even the appeal of the appeal – against a decision that
had been taken in a different department in another part
of the BBC. When I read the case notes and saw that it was
about one employee getting drunk and punching their

manager, or another biting someone's ear, I wondered why the consequence hadn't been instant dismissal, instead of which the puncher or biter was still on full or half pay a year or two later. Equally daft were those disputes which should have been nipped in the bud by a manager telling two members of staff to grow up or get out – but that's now defined as bullying and intimidation.

When travelling to different parts of the UK to hear these appeals, I would be accompanied by a colleague from HR, whose job it was to make sure I followed the rules and didn't succumb to any incredulous outbursts that might hand the union rep yet another reason to prolong the procedure. It gave me a glimpse into the mindset of such colleagues. On one such trip, my HR minder and I found ourselves killing time at an airport when our flight had been delayed. After a full eight hours of holding my tongue in a hot conference room, I was in the mood for a cold pint, but my minder showed a greater degree of professionalism in declining alcohol when on duty and, instead, made a beeline for the airport eatery. He was a big man and I doubted my ability to strong-arm him to the bar, so I followed. It was one of those cafeterias where a limited range of meals was served from big aluminium troughs kept warm under orange lamps. While I made a quick choice of chilli con carne, my travelling companion hovered over the chip urn, finally asking the chef-cum-server if those were 'fresh chips'.

'Yes, they were made today.'
'But how long ago? How fresh exactly?'
'I dunno, mate. About an hour ago.'
'Hmm. Not exactly fresh then.'

'Look,' said the chef, 'I don't know what you mean. Do you want me to go and make a new batch of chips just for you?'

'If it's not too much trouble, then yes.'

With some sighing and muttering, the chef stormed into his kitchen to do just that while we found a table. I brought with me my blobs of spiced mince and rice and began to tuck in. Between mouthfuls I asked about the fuss with the chips.

'Oh, Jeff, surely you're aware of my reputation?'

I shook my head.

He then told me that every lunchtime, the BBC canteen staff would allow him to sample one or two of the chips to check that they had been freshly fried. If they didn't pass muster, he would walk away. This sounded harmless, if slightly eccentric, but there was more to come.

'I got myself into a bit of bother recently,' he admitted, 'because I had a dispute with my local chip shop. It's a really good chippy, Jeff. One of the best.'

He mentioned the name of the chippy in question. I knew it and agreed with his assessment. They made damn fine fish and chips there.

'Trouble is,' he continued, 'I like my chips really fresh; *really* fresh. So, I'd go in there and wait until they put a new load in the fryer. If they offered to serve me before that, I'd would let someone else take my place in the queue.'

'I see.'

'Anyway, the boss of that chippy caught me doing this one day and asked me what I was up to. I explained that I liked my chips fresh and was prepared to wait.'

'And?'

'And the boss got really miffed. He said *all* his chips were fresh and that I could either eat the chips that were ready, or I could leave and never come back. "Take it or leave it," he said.'

'So, you left it?'

'Yes, of course I did. Because, Jeff, I like my chips fresh.'

'Yes, you've said.'

'But that gave me a huge problem. That was my favourite shop, Jeff. They were my favourite chips. But now I was banned from the place.'

'So, what did you do? Go back and apologise?'

'Of course not. I had nothing to be sorry about. What I did, Jeff, was I would go to the shop and stand outside. If I saw customers going in, I'd give them some money and ask them to get me some chips too. They could keep the change if they could keep a secret.'

I told him this story was starting to sound a bit dodgy: he sounded like one of those kids who waited outside shops and asked adults to go in and buy them booze.

'I know, Jeff, I know. Not good. So, after a month or two ...'

'Sorry. A *month* or two?'

'Yes, after a couple of months, I would go into the actual shop with a friend, a grown-up friend, a pal, and I'd let *him* buy the chips while I sort of loitered about behind him. I was testing the water, you see, wondering if they would recognise me.'

'Did they?'

'Not sure, but they didn't ask me to leave. So, I waited another month or so and then I summoned up the courage to buy the chips myself. I was as nervous as hell, I can tell you.'

'I can imagine. I'm nervous just thinking about it. And now?'

He smiled.

'Now, everything's fine. I get my chips there now and again, but I've also got another source. I bought one of those shallow fryers. Oh my god, Jeff, you should try it. The chips are delicious and you use hardly any oil at all.'

As his mouth started to water, a waiter appeared with the newly fried chips and placed the plate on the table with a little more force than was necessary: not quite a slam, but perhaps a distant relative of one, certainly in the extended family of slams. My minder began to munch merrily as my thoughts turned to so many protracted disciplinary processes and I wondered if I now had the first clue as to why the BBC's HR department had so much trouble in resolving disputes. Months of wrangling over buying a bag of chips? It was no wonder people used to think that a job at the BBC was a job for life. With so much hesitancy, with so many loopholes and appeals processes, I'm surprised anyone ever lived long enough to lose their job.

24.

HOW I LOST MY JOB

In my first few months working in Selkirk, I met the BBC's long-serving Training Officer, Bob Wood, and asked him the secret of his survival.

'Keep your head down,' was his advice.

Bob was the man who taught new recruits how to cut quarter-inch tape without also slicing an artery at the same time. When tape and razor blades were a thing of the past, he introduced us to the wonders of digital editing on systems like Pro Tools and Sadie, and we became adept at recognising a superfluous breath just by looking at the shape of an orphaned waveform. He had seen various generations of kit come and go, just as he had seen various BBC bosses come and go – sometimes of their own volition; sometimes kicking and screaming.

'Keep your head down,' he repeated. 'Well below the parapet.'

Although I took on board his hints and tips about mixers, faders and the complexities of editing in 16-track stereo, I wasn't good about keeping my head down or winding my neck in. When I had to spend hours to get to a meeting in Glasgow or London, I didn't want to just sit there, say nothing and then trek home again. I never felt I spoke just for the sake of speaking (gum-bumping at the BBC being the root cause of so many over-running meetings), and I tried to be supportive when a colleague offered some ideas, solutions or dazzling new insights. There were also times, especially in London meetings, when I felt obliged to offer a word of caution or an opposing viewpoint if I felt some strategy was likely to play badly in Scotland, or harm our production base in some way. Although I saw myself as the gentle voice of reason, I suspect others saw me as a scary Rab C. Nesbit figure, down from Glasgow to thump the table and demand transmitter capacity with menaces.

When I openly disagreed with the then Director of Radio – a brilliant champion of all things radio and self-assured in her opinions – I felt all eyes upon me. My tentative 'I'm not sure that would be the best way to run the in-house commissioning process' was probably perceived as 'Come ahead, hen, if you think you're hard enough.'

Another piece of advice had once been given to me by Ken MacQuarrie, who told me: 'Jeff, if you're ever in a big BBC meeting and someone asks you to give your honest opinion, always assume it's a trap. Don't do it.'

I wish I had remembered that thing about the trap, because I was often given ample opportunities to put my foot in it.

As the BBC secured another Royal Charter – effectively a Government licence to keep going for ten more years – there came the inevitable game of musical chairs at the top of the organisation. James Purnell became the new Director of Radio and Music and then advertised for a Director of Radio (yes, you're reading this correctly) to run the network radio stations. Happily, Bob Shennan got that job. Ken MacQuarrie was now the new Director of Nations and Regions and that created a vacancy for his old job running BBC Scotland. The hot favourite was Donalda MacKinnon, but others – mainly from the finance and operations side of the business – also applied.

Donalda encouraged me to submit an application on the basis that there should be more candidates with a production background. I did so, but my heart wasn't really in it. I know that's easy to say now, but in truth, although I could imagine myself doing the job, I couldn't imagine myself enjoying it. It was another step further away from the creative side and I could see I would have to put in a lot of hours glad-handing with politicians and sometimes defending the indefensible. Nevertheless, I was interviewed and thought I made a good fist of my presentation as I talked about the plans for a new television channel and how we could divert cash into making quality comedy and drama, developing a new generation of writers and performers, while spending smaller sums migrating some panel games and discussion formats from radio to the screen.

I pointed to the dangers of assuming that the news team could be left alone to deliver the new nine o'clock programme, because if it was to be successful, it would need some new thinking and fresh ideas. All of this seemed to be going down well and the interview panel, which was chaired by Tim Davie – one of the DG's right-hand men – seemed engaged. But then Tim asked me what I had thought of how BBC News had covered the European referendum and ... well, I gave an honest opinion.

I said there had been far too much of a focus on the big personalities in the campaign – Boris Johnson, Nigel Farage, etc. – and not enough explanation and analysis of the possible outcomes, or the different issues that might arise during any exit from the European Union. I talked about the work of Richard North, who had for many years been mapping out the twelve-year timescale that would be required to disentangle the UK from various treaties. I mentioned the impact on North Sea fishing rights and that, in most of the coverage, there seemed to be a tacit acceptance that protectionism was bad, rather than another economic strategy that needed to be explained.

When I finished, the smiles were gone and Tim Davie said my views on BBC News were 'pretty damning' and now he worried that I might not show the collective responsibility required for such a top job. Maybe he was right, but I always felt I had made my criticisms internally, rather than shouted them from the rooftops in newspaper interviews as other high-profile BBC figures had been allowed to do. In any case, I was happy enough when Donalda got the job as Director of BBC Scotland and then, as everyone had predicted, Ewan Angus won through to be the new Head of Multi-Platform Commissioning in her new structure, and Pauline Law would be the new Head of Production. Naturally, that had made me question the future viability of my own job, but time and again, Donalda assured me that, although my responsibilities might change, the Head of Radio figure was too important to lose.

I didn't see how this would work. I'd always thought it important to have a close relationship with the programme-makers and be part of the creative process. Experience over the years had taught me how frustrating it could be when departments as important as News and Sport worked to a different set of priorities. Creating more distance between the commissioner and the producers might have been logical in the business sense and might have worked well for television, but it was not a practical way to run a radio station. Retaining a Head of Radio within this new structure, I argued, just didn't make sense.

Finally, Donalda agreed. Hey, hand me a mirror so I can watch me slap myself on the forehead because this is where you came in ... and this is where I start to go out.

I talked it through with Anne and we took Rascal for a walk on Rosemarkie Beach as we came to a decision. As soon as that was made, I felt my stress dissolve and I knew it was the right one. I took a deep gulp of fresh air, let my gaze roam beyond the sand and out in to the choppy waters of the North Sea. There was no sign of those elusive dolphins, just the billowing white clouds of condensation emanating from the Norbord wood-processing factory on the other side of the firth. When they come to make the animated version of this book, I'll suggest those clouds form the image of a thumbs-up.

I called friends to tell them about my decision.

'Sleep on it,' Colin Paterson advised, 'and then call Kenny to see if there are opportunities with him at Nations and Regions.'

That wasn't a bad idea. The next morning, I put in a call to Ken MacQuarrie's office and asked if I could have an appointment to discuss my future. I hoped his PA would hear the urgency in my voice and, sure enough, just five days later, I was put straight through. By this time, I had already decided I'd be leaving, but I took the call just in case Kenny was going to surprise me with some lucrative offer.

'Hallo, Jeff,' he began. 'Now I want you to know that I'm approaching this conversation as a coach and mentor.'

This wasn't sounding good.

Kenny advised me to make sure my CV was up to date and said some encouraging things about how I could do anything I put my mind to. He himself, he continued, was now at a stage of life when he was going to do a lot more things for himself.

'I'm learning to fly a plane,' he told me, 'and to play the violin.'

'What, simultaneously?' I asked, but he didn't hear the question and continued to talk about his own life choices. There was no talk about a new job for me and, after twenty minutes, he brought the call to an end by telling me that he would do some thinking and that I should do some thinking too. I agreed to start my thinking immediately. He didn't put a timescale on his thinking. I was smiling. It really was time to go.

There's a training course for everything at the BBC and there's even one on how to leave it. I signed up for the day-long 'Leaving the BBC' seminar thinking it would offer psychological tips on how to adjust back into civilian life. When curious colleagues asked me about it, I said, straight-faced, that it involved instructions for senior managers on how to book their own taxis once they no longer had a personal assistant. Such was the generally accepted view of management as pampered incompetents that few realised I was joking. In fact, the course was more about *taxes* than *taxis*, but it was a good excuse for a trip to London, and it was the first time I had ever been in the famous Council Chamber at Broadcasting House. That room with its renovated art-deco styling, wood panelling and portraits of former Directors General should have had a sombre aura of history, but was rather ruined by the insertion of modern office furniture, plasma screen TVs and an empty Pepsi can on the mantelpiece, just below the gilt-framed painting of John Reith. You could tell standards were slipping – there was no fruit.

There were about twelve of us on the course that day and the group was evenly split between those of us who were looking forward to life after Auntie and others who felt they had been pushed out too early and were fretting about the fate of the teams and departments they would leave behind. One man said he was keen to get out of BBC News because morale was now at rock bottom. A female colleague from the Children's TV department was particularly anxious and I found myself, in the coffee breaks, trying to calm and console her with a vision of freedom and future opportunities that even I began to find convincing.

The speakers were experts on everything – pensions, mortgages, jobseekers' allowances – and there was a lively discussion (though I suspect this wasn't meant to be part of the curriculum) on the odds of hitting the jackpot in the National Lottery compared with winning £50 a week with the online betting site Paddy Power. I emerged at five o'clock brimming with all sorts of useful knowledge about retirement trusts and investments, which I had mostly forgotten by the time I made it back to Oxford Circus tube station. But I did buy a lottery ticket and won a life-changing £6 the following Saturday.

I do think it's a pity there isn't a different kind of BBC departure course, because I've seen so many people do it badly over the years. If they asked me to design it, the course would cover the etiquette of leaving, maintaining self-respect and reputation-management. I might even chuck in a parable from the Bible – that one about Jesus doing pay negotiations in the vineyard perhaps. From my point of view, I'd had almost twenty-five years at the Beeb, had received a salary akin to that of a Scottish head teacher, and was very grateful for the experiences I'd had and the friends I'd made. Apart from those few months of temporary insanity, I had loved the job. Also, it was my choice to leave. But I've seen others, even highly paid presenters, look at things very differently when told their contracts wouldn't be renewed. Instead of counting the loot they'd accumulated from licence-fee payers over the years, they'd rant bitterly about the years of service they'd given to the organisation, and phrases such as 'kick in the teeth' often come into play. Then there is a drunken leaving do with an ill-tempered speech and boat-burning jokes. Never good.

Some presenters had been known to make their unhappiness known to the audience when on air. It was before my time, but stories are still told of the Radio Scotland presenter who punctuated his final broadcast with pleas to the listeners to write to the station boss and persuade him to change his mind. 'Remember, it's your BBC,' he told them. Afterwards – and I suppose this does qualify as a bit of reputation-management, albeit as an afterthought – he walked into the studio's control cubicle and wordlessly removed the tape that contained the only recording of the show. It was never seen or heard of again.

Worse still are the top-flight managers who signal their departure up to a year in advance and then begin a nationwide or global tour to thank staff and say goodbye. I suspect some of this comes about because their successor wants them out of the way while they are picking up the threads of the new job. These farewell tours often involve a white-linen sit-down dinner in each of the main BBC buildings, or else a lunch at one of the fanciest restaurants in town. No one really likes attending and if the departing guest of honour opts to be indiscreet about their senior colleagues, it can be a very awkward conversation for those of us left behind. If invited, we attend these posh dinners out of a sense of respect and obligation or, at worst, because of that old adage about turning up at a person's funeral just to make sure they are really dead and the coffin lid has been nailed down.

When, some years back, the role of Head of Nations and Regions was abolished as part of the cost-cutting slimdown of top management (the role has since been reinstated), the ousted Head embarked on one of these sunset road-trips against a backdrop of press stories describing his '£886k pay-off'. This became a case study for the National Audit Office and resulted in a capping of subsequent redundancy deals for the rest of us. As we sat there of an evening sipping wine and listening to his reminiscences, I wondered if I was alone in recalling the speech he had once given to BBC Scotland staff way back in the days of Queen Margaret Drive, when he'd told an audience that included junior researchers, producers and editors that we, the BBC, were paying ourselves too much compared with others in the public sector. I didn't bring it up.

When I had made my decision to leave, I worked out a timetable for my exit that would allow Donalda MacKinnon, as the new Director of BBC Scotland, enough time to complete her restructuring process. Some of my duties as Head of Radio would be absorbed by a new Head of Production and the rest by an Executive Editor for Commissioning Radio and Music. This last role had yet to be advertised and the recruitment and appointment process took months to complete. The restructuring plans were then delayed further because Ewan Angus, who had been appointed as the new Head of Commissioning, had a rethink and decided to take a redundancy deal. I did wonder if my happy evangelising about my forthcoming freedom had had an influence on his decision, but I refuse to take any blame.

In the meantime, I worked in that strange period of limbo where I could get on with day-to-day duties such as ensuring programmes were compliant with editorial guidelines, but recused myself from any meetings that dealt with future plans beyond the end of the year.

Responsibility for staffing issues was transferred to the new production unit, but some producers and researchers still sought out my advice on how they should manage their careers. Now that I had no vested interest beyond friendship, I guess my advice was worth hearing. Irene Jones, my personal assistant, noticed that my diary was starting to thin out, and those remaining meetings I did attend had an air of unreality about them. I began, in my mind, to create distance between myself and the organisation. I sat through a Business Continuity Meeting in which all I could think was that it was such a dull name for a meeting, about the resilience in our systems in the event of a major power failure, or a successful cyber-attack. If they'd called it 'Managing Meltdown', I thought, people might have been more engaged in the potential for disaster.

Like the flashback sequence for a drowning man, I was suddenly having odd and random encounters with former colleagues. On a street in Finnieston, I met news reporter Glenn Cooksley, who had been my opposite number in Dumfries when I started work for the BBC in Selkirk. I was reminded of the time, after a few drinks, when we had developed an idea for a pornographic radio station called Radio Erotica – a plan that I thought of resurrecting after the success of the *Fifty Shades of Grey* books and the acceptance of soft porn in mainstream culture. Maybe it should be a podcast. All I needed was a sponsor.

Hurrying through Queen Street Station I saw John Thomson, a former producer in Topical Radio. Working, in recent years as an indie, he had produced what I'd described at the time as a 'life-saving' documentary on prostate cancer. I remembered telling him that his programme was in the best traditions of public-service broadcasting. Now, having switched jobs a few times himself, he advised me to keep it together during those final weeks and warned of the 'dangerous high' of being demob happy that could make people do odd things. I promised him I wouldn't blow it.

I was determined to go out with dignity. On the other hand, doing odd things had become the habit of a lifetime.

I began tentatively to think about the future. Friends like Claire Dean from Clyde and investigative reporter Eamonn O'Neill had both translated their careers in journalism into lecturing at universities. They gave me some advice about the academic world, including how I should dress! I was also contacted by Jenny Crowe at the Platform Arts Project in Easterhouse, asking if I'd be interested in joining their board. I'd met Jenny when she was the Artist in Residence at BBC Scotland. We had shared similar childhood memories of holidays in Carnoustie and Broughty Ferry ... and now Jenny was working in the very place where I had grown up. A recent visit to Platform had left me impressed with the changes happening in Easterhouse and the ambition of the arts workers there. Since Dad's death I'd had few reasons to go back to the neighbourhood of my childhood, but I liked the idea of keeping a connection.

I also got a call asking if I would host the Scottish Comedy Awards in Edinburgh. I accepted in the full knowledge that they must already have been turned down by ten other people, and also knowing I would get a verbal roasting from just about every comedian who took to the stage, because they would only remember the programmes I hadn't commissioned or had dropped from the schedule, or the panel shows on which they had not been invited to appear. This prediction turned out to be uncannily accurate, although I hadn't reckoned on being presented with a rubber phallus in the first five minutes.

Planning and commissioning for Radio Scotland's Christmas and Hogmanay schedule would be my last major piece of work and then, at the Celtic Connections Festival, my annual speech at the Young Traditional Musician Final would be my last public outing. This would go out live on the night and I kept hinting to the Press Office that I might use the airtime to tell a few home truths about the BBC.

'Just joking,' I said, 'just joking.'

I was delighted when Gareth Hydes won through to be the new executive in charge of radio commissioning, but his duties at BBC Children in Need meant he couldn't start until the turn of the year, so for a few more months I retained responsibility for the relationship with the independent production companies. Reviewing my plans for the Christmas schedule, I felt it had far too much nostalgia, although two documentaries from Nick Low's Demus Productions turned out to be real gems: one was on the author Alistair MacLean; and the other told the inside story – drug deaths and all – of the Average White Band. I made a trip to Lochwinnoch to meet with Lyn McNicol and Laura Jackson, authors and, in Laura's case, illustrator of the *Badger the Mystical Mutt* children's books. Their story of abandoning the rat race to follow their dream was inspiring and I called Richard Melvin at Dabster Productions to suggest this might make a documentary for the festive season: as a contemporary story it would help dilute the preponderance of nostalgia. He agreed and this, my final commission for BBC Radio Scotland, turned out to be a cracking listen.

As my time and power was running out, I also wanted to finalise a deal for Grant Stott, the popular Edinburgh presenter who had decided to part company with Radio Forth. On and off over the years, Grant and I had talked about him joining Radio Scotland, but I had never been able to find enough slots in the schedule which would have made it worth his while to leave commercial radio. I would have been happy for him to join the BBC while still retaining a relationship with Radio Forth – perhaps he could do evening or weekend programmes for us, and the breakfast show for them – but the Bauer Group, who owned stations like Clyde and Forth, didn't like their presenters moonlighting with others. As soon as I heard that he was a free agent, I swooped, and over lunch we hammered out a deal that involved him presenting programmes about his collection of vinyl records, hosting editions of the afternoon arts show and chairing a new comedy panel game, *Stop the Press*. No sooner had we shaken hands on this than Grant read in the papers about my plan to leave the BBC. Happily, I managed to persuade him that he should still make the leap, gambling that my successor would also realise that such a seasoned and popular presenter was a natural fit for the audience that Radio Scotland needed to keep.

Newspaper coverage of my departure tended to conflate my decision 'to quit' with plans BBC Scotland had been drawing up for an additional digital radio station offering music and cultural content. This had been my pet project ever since the demise of the archive Zones, but the *Herald* reporter got into a fankle and implied I was leaving because of plans to completely remove music from Radio Scotland. I wrote to clarify the position and that was published.

Given my career-long aversion to cosying up with politicians, I was surprised and pleased when the MSP Pauline McNeill, tabled a motion in the Scottish Parliament thanking me for my work and, in particular, Radio Scotland's support for the music scene in Scotland. The latter, it has to be said, was mainly down to the expertise and enthusiasm of our music producers in Glasgow and Aberdeen.

All that was left was to organise a bit of a knees-up, write a farewell speech and then hand back my ID card. My termination date would be 7th April, but the HR department discovered that in twenty-five years, I had accumulated almost six weeks of long-service leave, which I had neglected to take. So, it was to be a Thursday night in February when Anne, Sarah and Alan joined me for the farewell party on the fifth floor of Pacific Quay.

Waiting there were friends and colleagues from just about every era of my career, and some of the students I had mentored along the way and who were now forging their own careers in broadcasting. Current members of the Executive Board were joined by former bosses such as Maggie Cunningham and ex-BBC Scotland Controller, John McCormick. Gareth Hydes, free from the clutches of Pudsey Bear, gave a gentle and touching speech about our past exploits together, and Colin Paterson – now the Editor of BBC Radio Wales – was characteristically mischievous, poking fun at my yo-yo dieting over the years and the trail of oatcake crumbs I tended to leave on my desk when trying to cut out pastries and biscuits. More poignantly he described how often I had told stories about my dad – a man, said Colin, he had never met, but felt he knew because of my vivid anecdotes. Similarly, Donalda gave an emotional welcome to my family and told how often I had talked about them over the years with obvious love and pride.

Then it was my turn to speak. The key elements here, I thought, were brevity and relevance. Many of us were still smarting from an event held a few weeks previously as part of the celebrations to mark our tenth year at Pacific Quay: a member of the new BBC Unitary Board in London had arrived and delivered a speech, mostly about himself, that lasted so long that by the time he finished it felt like it might now be time to celebrate eleven years at PQ. *The shorter, the better*, I thought.

I patted my jacket pocket to make sure I had my glasses, unfolded my two sheets of A4 and made my way to the front to deliver the speech that I had been crafting for weeks: a speech full of memories, profound thoughts about broadcasting, heartfelt thanks to individual friends and colleagues. As I stared down at the blurred words, I reached for my glasses, only to find I was holding my sunglasses instead of my more vital Poundland readers. I thought of putting them on for the cheap laugh, but didn't.

I pressed on regardless, remembering some of what I had wanted to say, forgetting loads more. Afterwards, I had to apologise to various people for my omissions, including my PA Irene, who had organised the party. Face-slap time again.

But, in truth, there were – and are – too many memories to recall and too many people to mention and to thank.

To do that properly, I'd have to write a book.

25.

AFTERLIFE

Anne had fretted about allowing Alan to make the train trip to Glasgow, but he was fourteen years old, travelling with a mate and wanted to spend the money and gift cards he had received for Christmas. I gave him a lift to Inverness station and we checked that all the services were on time, despite the winter gales the previous night. I waved him off and drove home. The phone was ringing when I walked through the door. Anne was in the shower and hadn't heard it. It was Alan. His voice was matter-of-fact.

'The train has crashed.'

'What?'

'Yep, it hit a tree near Dunkeld. There are ambulances outside.'

Two people had been injured but luckily not seriously. Alan and his friend had been sitting a few rows away but had felt the train brake as the driver spotted the tree on the line. It could have been a lot worse. Some windows had caved in and there had been some screaming, but he was unharmed. I hesitated before asking the next question.

'Can I tell the newsroom?'

When Anne emerged from the shower I described what had happened and she gave me that 'told-you-so' look. She had to make several calls before she got hold of Alan again. He had been liaising with the BBC newsroom in Glasgow, giving an interview for the *John Beattie Show* on Radio Scotland and agreeing to a TV interview at Queen Street station, where a crew from *Reporting Scotland* had arranged to meet him off the replacement train. He called home afterwards and told us he had been given a free cup of hot chocolate. Then he went shopping.

That morning I had arranged to meet Danny Gallagher, who was now running Moray Firth Radio. He gave me a tour of the station. Some things had changed, but not much. As we passed the news desk I mentioned the train crash. Danny hadn't heard about it and the story wasn't running on their bulletins. Alan had scooped them, and the next morning all the newspapers were using his quotes from his BBC interviews. That was it for him. The news bug had bitten and in the next few years he sought out work placements on *The Inverness Courier* and *Highland News*, and then enrolled on the Journalism course at Glasgow Caledonian University. He was soon getting paid shifts at newspaper and radio stations, including at Capital Radio in Glasgow and at Radio Clyde. It was odd to think of him walking into the same newsroom where I had worked thirty years before. I wondered if those old telephone directories were still there. It was even odder when he called to tell me that *The Scottish Sun* had asked him to do some video work for their website and social media which involved recording interviews in a strip club. Sarah, meanwhile, qualified as a hospital radiographer and has long grown weary of my Dad jokes about her 'having a bone to pick' with people, or 'seeing right through them'.

The summer of 2018 had been one of the best in years and, in the months after leaving the BBC, I had settled into a routine of walking, writing and lunching. I converted Sarah's old bedroom into a study and Rascal slept at my feet as I hammered away at the keyboard. If I paused too long, his eyes would open and he would raise his head, doubtless wondering if a biscuit break was in the offing. With Sarah and Alan now both living in Glasgow, Rascal had spared us from a completely empty nest, but he began to slow down. At first the vet diagnosed arthritis, and painkillers seemed to work. A few weeks later, he had a seizure and another vet discovered tumours. She told us it was time to say goodbye. We stroked his soft fur as she put him to sleep then we cried our eyes out for a week.

In July, Anne and I spent a week in Prague. My search for the offices of Radio Prague was half-hearted and fruitless and, besides, I'm not sure anyone there would have been interested in hearing how I'd once entered one of their competitions and won a record. Since the fall of the Soviet Union and the Velvet Revolution, things were very different in Prague: Franz Kafka was being celebrated in the form of a huge, spinning bust of his head – a bloke on a block; Communism was confined to history and to a fantastic museum which told of the years of repression. As we wandered around, we came to a small room kitted out like a teenager's bedroom. There was something familiar about that single bed, the small desk and the transistor radio set sitting on top. It could have been my bedroom when I was a teenager. No doubt, as I was listening to Radio Prague in Glasgow, some teenage boy or girl in this city had been tuning into the BBC or Radio Free Europe. For me, radio had been fun ... for people behind the Iron Curtain it had been a vital source of information.

'Do you miss it?' people ask me. 'Do you miss working in radio?'

I give my stock answer. 'I miss the people,' I tell them. 'I miss friends and colleagues.'

The answer seems to satisfy them, but it's not really true. I miss spotting ideas and stories and sending them to relevant programme teams, but those friends and colleagues that I want to see, I make the effort to do so. They like to tell me what's happening at work, moan about some management decision or describe their excitement about a new programme idea or a commission from Radio 4. Sometimes when they talk about a particular editorial problem or a staffing crisis, I feel momentarily anxious, until I remember it has nothing to do with me and I don't have to go into the office on Monday morning and sort it. I can zone out. All I have to do is listen to the radio and enjoy it.

And that's always been the best part.

APPENDIX:
THE GREEN LIGHT ZONE

There's no doubt the BBC Radio Scotland schedule is driven by the big daily strands like *Good Morning Scotland, Kaye Adams, John Beattie, Out of Doors* and *Sportsound*. But one of the joys of having been a commissioner is that I can look back fondly on so many other programmes and projects I've 'green-lit' over the years and stack them into my top fifty alongside those where I was personally involved in the production. You could ask me to write this list in a week or a month's time and it would probably change. Some other gem would come to mind and I would kick myself for not including it. In other words, it's not a definitive list: just a damn fine selection of my favourites ... in alphabetical order.

ALISTAIR MACLEAN: MASTER STORYTELLER
Greg Hemphill told the story of the best-selling author, using revealing archive recordings of the man himself alongside contributions from colleagues, friends and family members.

ANOTHER COUNTRY ... WITH RICKY ROSS
A programme that has rightly garnered awards and tributes from around the world. Ricky's respect for the craft of musicians and songwriters shines through in every interview.

BBC RADIO SCOTLAND LISTENERS' CHRISTMAS LUNCH
We did this for two or three years. Listeners entered a ballot

for tickets and spent a jingle jolly afternoon sitting beside one of twelve Radio Scotland presenters. Some found these encounters with the audience invigorating and inspiring. Others ... not so much.

BBC RADIO SCOTLAND MUSIC EXTRA
Our eight-day pilot, demonstrating how an additional music and culture station for Scotland would actually sound.

BBC RADIO SCOTLAND YOUNG TRADITIONAL MUSICIAN OF THE YEAR
Each year we seemed to crank up the pressure on the young finalists. We made it a live event, then we added television cameras and social media. But year after year, the talent on stage just blew us away, especially the bagpipers.

BLACK STREET
I was always asking our Music team to tell us if we were missing any genres or overlooking any scene in Scotland. Laura McCrum presented this series on black music which, as it happens, featured one of the first ever radio performances by Emeli Sandé.

BRAINWAVES
Nothing to do with my ill-fated TV game show mentioned in Chapter 11. Pennie Latin presented this weekly programme exploring the latest advances in scientific research, particularly at Scottish universities. Her description of the cadavers in a pathology lab still haunts me.

BREAKING THE NEWS
Months after the independence referendum, the political landscape in Scotland was ripe for comedy. Des Clarke

presented this multi-award-winning panel show which, as well as being very funny, also gave airtime to a new generation of male and female stand-up comedians.

Burns Online
Producers David Batchelor and Esme Kennedy arranged for all 716 works of Robert Burns to be recorded and placed in an online library (still available). Among the many famous names invited to record a poem or song was HRH Prince Charles.

Classics Unwrapped
Producer Lindsay Pell developed this format which allowed us to showcase the classical music scene in Scotland and abroad. Jamie MacDougall brought his sense of fun and enthusiasm to a genre which can sometimes be viewed as elitist and unwelcoming.

Dad Made Me Laugh
Inverness producer Mike Walker made this series in which we heard from the sons and daughters of famous comedians. The series has been repeated many times on BBC Radio 4 Extra. It takes the concept of 'dad jokes' to a whole new level.

Dean Friedman's Real American Folk
One of my early commissions. Richard Melvin travelled along the Hudson River Line in New York State to talk to Dean Friedman, who presented two series of programmes on American folk music and the stories of his own childhood – proving there was much more to Dean than his hit song 'Lucky Stars'.

Desperate Fishwives
Margaret-Anne Docherty produced multiple series of this Aberdeen-based sketch show, featuring the comedy troupe

The Flying Pig. It was a huge hit with listeners because it was so different from Glasgow humour.

Digging Up Your Roots

I had long questioned the appeal of a programme on genealogy and family ancestry, but the popularity of the TV show *Who Do You Think You Are?* made me realise I was wrong. The team in Aberdeen did a fine job with this series.

Dress Circle

Billy Differ, trouble-shooter for the Cameron Mackintosh organisation, is full of hilarious stories about backstage life in London's West End. In this series he played his own favourite songs from the shows and interviewed stars of stage and screen.

Ellis Island

Comedy actress Elaine MacKenzie Ellis teamed up with Des Clarke and a series of special guests for a lively sketch show recorded in front of an audience at Pacific Quay.

Feeling Kind of Funny

At the Scottish Storytelling Centre in Edinburgh, Julia Sutherland introduced comedians whose material was inspired by the darker episodes in their lives. Laughter as therapy was the key message of this and subsequent series exploring the relationship between comedy and mental health.

Fifty Years, Fifty Lives

A brilliant series produced by the BBC Radio Scotland Diversity Team, led by Norwegian-born Margaret Telfer. Stories of immigration, prejudice and acceptance, as people who had settled in Scotland described their experiences over a fifty-year span.

Free Falling

A sitcom about Raymond Swann's mid-life crisis, played in the early series by James MacPherson and later by John Gordon Sinclair. I was laughing out loud when I read the first scripts. I suspect the theme meant more to me than others.

Give Me a Voice

Suzy Beaumont was the main producer here in a series in which people who felt their lives and experiences were being marginalised were given time and space to tell their stories. It included an award-winning episode on male domestic violence.

Jail Mates

Comedian Gary Little – who really had done some time behind bars – teamed up with Julia Sutherland for a sitcom about a prisoner and single mother becoming pen-pals. Ironically, the prisoner seemed to have more freedom than the mum.

Legend of the Holyrood Vampires

A four-part comedy drama for Halloween week, written by A.L. Kennedy and produced by Gus Beattie. The story of a vampire hunter in nineteenth-century Edinburgh had a cast that included Karen Dunbar, Ford Kiernan and Greg McHugh.

Let's Do the Show Right Here

If you needed to raise funds for a good cause in your community, why not put on a show? Radio Scotland supplied the compere and a celebrity guest, then we told the story of your cause and how you put the show together.

Lulu of a Kid
Lulu's story of her Glasgow childhood and her rise to fame in the sixties was brought to life by our Radio Drama team.

Magnetic Memories
A fascinating series in which we encouraged listeners to unearth old audio recordings from their attic: reel-to-reel tapes and cassettes. You heard voices from the past talking about family life in Scotland.

Morton at Midnight
I think this was Tom Morton's fourth reincarnation on Radio Scotland. His late-night show, presented live from his croft-house in Shetland, allowed him to share his passion for music, interspersed with stories of life in the Northern Isles.

Pandemic: Scotland and the Flu
The dramatic story of how Scotland was affected by the flu pandemic in 1918 and how it killed more people than in the First World War.

Passport to Kelso
A year before the independence referendum, producer David Stenhouse went to Kelso High School to record the result of a mock vote. The issues highlighted by the pupils mirrored those we heard in the real campaign. The Kelso result, though, was a decisive 'Yes'.

SoundTown
Each year, Radio Scotland would be invited to a secondary school in Scotland. We would install a radio studio and spend twelve months working with pupils, staff and parents

on a range of projects involving just about every department at the station.

Sportsound: Open All Mics
Sport Editor Tom Connor came to me with the idea of allowing our pundits and commentators to chip in immediately something happened at any of the football matches we were covering. Richard Gordon had the role of ringmaster, making sure listeners were kept abreast of the action as it was happening.

Stan Laurel's Glasgow
Producer Dave Flynn shared my love of Laurel and Hardy, and in this programme he told the story of Stan's early life in Glasgow and his first performances at the city's Panopticon theatre. Alex Norton presented the programme.

Stark Talk
Edi Stark is one of the best interviewers on *any* BBC radio station and has won more Sony Radio Academy Awards than any other presenter on Radio Scotland. Meticulous research and courageous questioning combine to produce compelling programmes, with interviewees usually uttering the phrase 'How on earth did you find out about that?' at least once in each programme.

Stuck: The Rise and Fall of Johnny Sellotape
A bit of self-indulgence here. I had fun scripting and playing a small role in this mockumentary as we used the fictional Johnny (famed for his jokeless comedy) to send up all those familiar stories of the Glasgow variety days and Clydeside humour.

The Book I've Yet to Write
So many people say they have a book in them, but simply don't have the time to sit down and write it. In this series we invited some famous people to save themselves the trouble and just tell us the synopsis.

The Cause
A series that required more than a few calls to Editorial Policy, as Billy Kay told the story of the independence movement and the history of the Scottish National Party.

The Day I Didn't Die
I produced the first series of this programme about people's near-death experiences, and the Inverness team revived it years later for another series. It did make you realise the fragility of life and encouraged you to stop and smell the roses.

The Dundee Ripper
Billy Kay in blood-curdling form as he told the story of the Dundee killer who was also suspected of being Jack the Ripper.

The Franz Kafka Big Band
Surreal, controversial and unlike any other comedy that had appeared on Radio Scotland, like a darker, edgier version of *The Goon Show*. Brilliant writing, performing and audio production combined to pop images in your mind that you can never unsee.

The Gorbals Vampire
I always claimed Halloween as a Scottish festival and insisted on some creepy content at the end of October. David

Stenhouse produced for us and Radio 4 this story of how rumours of a vampire with iron teeth scared Glasgow schoolchildren in the 1950s and led to a change in the censorship rules around comic books. Novelist Louise Welsh presented the programme.

THE JAZZ HOUSE

The jazz show for people who thought they didn't like jazz. Stephen Duffy and guests presented a mix of live music and discs in a format that was designed as a summer 'filler' but was so good it ran for years.

THE LONG SHADOW OF THE WORLD'S END

In-depth research and quality journalism from the Edinburgh Features team in a two-part programme fronted by Edi Stark. The World's End murders had become a cold case until new techniques in DNA analysis led to the identity of the killer.

THE LOST LETTERS

Freelance reporter Paul English discovered a treasure trove in his attic: letters he had received from pen-pals since his early childhood. He tracked down those pals to find out if they remembered him and how their lives had turned out.

THE MUSIC MATCH

Nick Low's Demus Productions brought this late-night music show to the airwaves and had a mandate to find new presentation talent for Radio Scotland. Over the years, different presenters – mainly female – were given a run of ten or more programmes to let us hear what they could do. Many went on to get a regular gig on Radio Scotland or other stations.

The Quay Sessions

'Build it and they will come,' I told the Music team as they set about constructing a stage in the BBC foyer at Pacific Quay, and then invited some top-class musicians and bands to perform in front of a small audience for radio, then online and then television.

The Quest of Donal Q

For a co-commission with Radio 4, Billy Connolly and Brian Cox were paired for this retelling of the Don Quixote story in a modern Scottish setting. Again, our Radio Drama team was in excellent form.

The Voice of Mickey Mouse

After months of negotiations with Disney, producer James Christie was able to tell the story of Dundee-born Jimmy MacDonald who, for forty years, was the voice of Mickey Mouse. Brian Cox presented the programme about this unassuming sound-effects supervisor whose career took an odd turn when he got a call from Walt Disney himself.

Time Travels

Comedian Susan Morrison has always had an interest in history, and this magazine format allows us to share her enthusiasm as she journeys around Scotland hearing stories of Scotland's past.

When Bossman Jay Lost His Ears

Jay Crawford is a bit of a legend in the world of Scottish radio. As a presenter and programme director at Radio Forth and Scot FM, he was forced to retire when he was diagnosed with a form of tinnitus that made him unable to listen to music. Producer Al Lorraine used his own skill for audio mixing to recreate what Jay was experiencing.

ZONES

Five online zones – Comedy, Classical, History, Celtic and Arts – each of them running twenty-four hours a day and using programmes from the vast archive available in our digital library. It was an early experiment in what could be achieved in the world of online radio. Producer Lizzy Clark used her experience with the archive to produce *The 4 O'Clock Show* for Radio 4 Extra.

AND FINALLY...

A special mention for a programme which must qualify as having the worst title I ever came up with. Designed as a summer filler in the break from the football season, the 'sport and food and music' chat show would feature the spouses, partners and girlfriends of well-known Scottish footballers. I imagined it as our version of *Loose Women*. I had suggested 'Wives with Knives' as the title. Then one of our editors expressed concern about that title because there had been a recent spate of stabbings in Glasgow. Panicked, I added an additional and safer item of cutlery and also wanted to flag up there would be music in the show.

And so, *Wives with Knives and Spoons and Tunes* hit the airwaves.

For just one series.

ABOUT THE AUTHOR

Jeff Zycinski is the eighth and youngest child of a Polish sailor who settled in Scotland after the Second World War and who met Jeff's mother in a Glasgow dance hall. Jeff was born in the city's Easterhouse housing estate in 1963. Despite its reputation, he describes his childhood there as idyllic and safe – probably because he had a sister and six older brothers looking out for him.

After leaving school, Jeff tried jobs as a postman, a shelf-stacker and a wages clerk in a colliery. Satisfied that he had explored the real world sufficiently, he enrolled at Glasgow's Central College of Commerce and then continued his studies at what is now Glasgow Caledonian University. He then spent a year at University College in Cardiff gaining a postgraduate diploma in Journalism.

Jeff worked as a news reporter for Moray Firth Radio in Inverness and Radio Clyde in Glasgow before joining the BBC in 1993. His previous writing has included the radio comedy *Stuck* and a series of monologues entitled *Teacake Tales*. He also wrote a daily online blog for the BBC website which is still available as archived content.

He married Anne, a research scientist, the same year he began work as BBC Radio Scotland's senior producer in Selkirk. They have two children, Sarah and Alan, and now live in Inverness with their dog, Scrabble.

Since leaving the BBC in 2018, Jeff has joined the board of the Platform arts group in Easterhouse and has taken up invitations to lecture at universities and colleges throughout Scotland.

Jeff describes his hobbies as walking, listening to audio books and yo-yo dieting.

You can find out more about the author and see photographs and video material relating to this book by visiting

TheRedLightZone.com